Youth Football Manual

By
Dan Nappi

Special thanks to
Dan Jr. and Wes Nappi for their
input and help on many levels.

Also thanks to
Brian Nappi for keeping it real
and helping me understand
hockey, icing and what
the heck is a crease.

ams
advanced | media | solutions
www.amsrabbit.com

I0144106

Copyright © 2009 by Dan Nappi
Published by Advanced Media Solutions
Salt Lake City, Utah

www.youthfootballmanual.com
coachnappi@yahoo.com

ISBN-13: 978-0-578-02028-0

Library of Congress Control Number: 2009903823

Caution
Football and all outdoor activities are by their nature potentially
hazardous and participants in such should and must assume the
responsibility for their own actions and safety. We cannot include
all the potential hazards and risks involved in this and any contact
sport; you should learn all you can before beginning this or any
sporting activity and take the necessary safety precautions.

Printed in the United States of America
2009

Contents

Introduction

This book is designed specifically for youth football. It will give you a great start to building your own program and help you through your first years in coaching. We have laid out a step-by-step plan that will guide you through the first things you will need to know to get started and take you all the way to your first game. This is not a book full of endless formations, countless plays and eight different defenses; there is already a book on that. This book is designed more on the concepts of football and the details on why plays work and why they don't. Having great plays is great only if you know when to use them and how. This program also includes a workbook you can fill in as you go along. The workbook will help you build your program the way you want and not just have a collection of plays and random stories about football that may or may not relate to what you want to do. There are endless points of view about football but yours is the only one that matters. Use what you can from all sources to build your own football team and let me just help you by teaching you how to develop drills, plays, defenses and all that goes with the game and that will be more valuable to you than having a book full of plays and defenses that you may never use.

We also offer a DVD with this program that will show you how some of the more difficult drills should be run. Sometimes you have to see it in action before you get the details of how the play or drill looks and works. There is also a lot more in the DVD that we couldn't put into words, it is so much better when you see it.

You can also join our team on-line and learn from coaches across the country on how they handle a problem in their league or with their teams. You can ask questions and add your own experiences to the host of feedback we get worldwide. You can access the message board and find out about other books and articles on football that have helped others with similar situations. Look at game film and great plays throughout the network.

Nothing About Football

Football is a very easy sport to play and to learn. You can take a few people, find some open grass and set up a game in about two minutes. That is why it always confounds me to see people try to make it so difficult. I hope with this program I can take the mystery out and put the fun back in, yes this is supposed to be fun not just for the players but for the coaches as well.

To start I would like to break it down into just two elements, offense and defense. On offense the objective is to move the ball down a one hundred yard field and into the end zone, for which your team is awarded six points. On the other side the defense is trying to prevent that from happening. But as you can tell if you have been involved in football in anyway there are as many ways to get that done, as there are head coaches and coordinators. In the past I have written books on football and filled them with a lot of plays, defenses, pictures and cute stories. However up until just recently I have discovered that those elements are such a small part of the game and it is more about the details and the psychological aspects. I have been very fortunate to be involved in winning programs all my life and then I was unfortunate to be involved with a very bad program. I took winning for granted until I got involved with that losing program and I had to take a step back and rethink my football I.Q. I was not happy about that at the time, but looking back, I now thank that inept head coach for teaching me the way not to do virtually everything.

Being around a losing program made me focus on why teams win and why they lose. Now I can tell you that it has very little to do with football and everything to do with people and their attitudes. Not to say that plays and defenses are not important but I want you to move the psychological part of the game up on your list of things to consider when teaching or playing football. One thing I have found to be very important is that winners are winners and losers are losers and never the two shall meet. There is a reason for that. Winners cannot stand to be around losers and losers cannot stand to be around winners, it makes them uncomfortable. (You can convert them to winners but you have to be strong and patient.) I am going to try to uncover some truths in this program that I hope you will find informative and fun.

I am not going to take credit for all there is in this program because most of what I learned I got from other people and situations. I was just fortunate to hang on to what worked and was able to alter it to fit my program.

First of all let me say that it's "my way or the highway" and there is no other way. One voice, one leader, you cannot have multiple leaders and multiple points of view. It does not work, (just look at the United States Congress.) Once my players and assistant coaches agree with that then I will listen to what they have to say. I have learned my best football from assistant coaches and players. I want to hear what they have to say even if I don't agree, it will sometimes trigger a thought and start me thinking and I put the two together and come up with something great. So keep your mind open and you will be surprised at what you can learn.

It is also very important to not get mad "stay cool man". If you call the wrong play or someone drops the ball, get over it, hanging on to negative just brings more negative. Move on to the next play or situation and never blame your players for anything particularly during a game. Everything bad that happens is your fault and everything good that happens is because they are awesome football players. Once you can understand this concept you are on your way to being a great coach. Remember they make all the great plays and you make all the bad calls.

If you want to get mad at someone try looking at yourself, you're their coach and if they screw up guess who their teacher is. Never talk bad about a player or let any team member talk bad about a player or coach for that matter. That will start a landslide of bad and will grow like a cancer until it undermines your entire program and leaves you with a mess you may not be able to recover from. "Nip it in the bud" as they say. This simply means to cut it out before it spreads. Work as a team after all that is what you are. If one looks bad it will show on the whole team. You can't build team spirit if they are working against each other and you certainly can't build a championship team that way. If you want a great team, one that can be champions then start by treating them like champions, make them feel like champions in everything you do and teach, be positive. "If you can believe it, then you can achieve it." Act, talk and do as champions do. Winners do not try to bring down their team mates, they try to help them and make them better. They realize that when the team does well then they all will benefit from it.

I followed a team this year that had a quarterback that was more interested in his own stats than his team. It showed in his play and in his actions on and off the field. When it came time for the big games on their schedule they lost every one of them. You could see in his performances that he was worried about how he would look if he threw an incomplete pass or interceptions and not what it would take to win the game. This was a good team and always finished at the top of their league, but the quarterback coach thought that the ability of the quarterback would overshadow his self-centeredness. However they found out by sad experience that the wrong attitude especially for the quarterback will destroy a team. Hopefully they learned that the right attitude will prove to be more valuable than the ability to throw an accurate pass.

There are always going to be things that go wrong during a game, don't dwell on it. Move off it as quickly as you can. I see a lot of coaches start yelling at their players and making big changes during a game. This is not going to work, if you haven't worked on it in practice you are not going to all of the sudden come up with this great plan and change everything and win the game. If they haven't worked on it all week you are not going to be able to shove it down their throat during a game. Not to say you can't make small adjustments during a game or at the half but redoing the entire defense because they scored a touchdown is not going to work. Don't laugh I've seen coaches try it. It does make me laugh, especially when it's the opposing team.

Mandatory play rule - don't you hate that phrase? Some football programs have a mandatory play rule that basically says that every player must play at least so many plays during a game and special teams does not count. If you do not have this rule skip this part but I have found a way around this little bump in the road. It's called offense. I can take a not-so-good player and put him on one side of the ball, then run to the other side. The same goes for a not-so-good receiver, you can bring him into a game and then run the ball. However I would like to tell you a little story that I found to be of great value to me through the years. I was coaching a team where

I had only thirteen players, that was the whole team. Some games I had to start with just ten players. Luckily the eleventh showed up before we were disqualified. Most of the time I had one guy on the bench. Well to make a short story long. I had a receiver that couldn't catch the ball and with no back up and no choice I started to work with this boy and came up with drills that would teach him the basics of receiving. Turns out he was afraid of being hit so we spent a lot of time on drills that got him hit a lot. First we started slow just short passes then longer and longer till he could hold onto the ball in a normal pass pattern. Then the fun started, I set up a line of defensive player to hit him after he caught the ball, soft at first then increasing the intensity as he got better. To my surprise it didn't take long till he was a receiver. The point is that we tend to forget the players that are not as good and give our time to the ones that are, but you may need them at some point so for their sake and yours don't leave them out. With all that said let's get into the game of football. I would like to give you an overview of this program and some of the areas I would like to cover.

Overview

In this program we will go over everything you will need to coach your own football team. Either on a little league level or as far up the ladder as you can convince an athletic director to let you have a shot. The program has been broken down into several sections to make it easy to go through and later to be used as a reference guide. You can go back to it if you feel the need. Sometimes you don't feel like it applies to you but then something happens and you need some direction or help. The DVD will give you more detail and additional information and is designed to go along with this book. All of these elements come together to give you a sound foundation to build your program on. The workbook is where you will put your notes as well as begin to build your program. When you find plays, formation or anything you want to keep, put that information in the workbook that is laid out so it follows this book and will become your playbook.

We will start by taking you through a step-by-step process as if you were starting a team for the first time. Use what you will and skip the things that don't apply to you. The first thing to decide is which offense, defense and special teams you want to run. In each section I will always give you an example, use it if you want, but remember what works for me may not necessarily work for you. You should develop your own as you go along.

I will go through having assistant coaches and how to manage them. We will go through a host of drills and the day-to-day activities of a perfect practice. Taking you through with a step-by-step plan starting with position names and numbers as well as the numbers of the holes and gaps. We will go over a few formations to give you a look at what can be done and to give you a starting point for you to begin building your team. All this will lead us into a game like situation where I will try to show you the when, where, why and who of a well-managed game.

I also put at the end of this book what I called random thoughts about football. It is just a few ideas I have collected over the years and felt they might be fun and maybe helpful.

Chapter One
Setting Up Your Offense

Before we get into the program I want to take a second and talk to you about assistant coaches. I love them, I need them, but they must be subject to the King, better known as "Head Coach." One voice, one leader, you cannot run a football program by committee. I do not mean you are to micro manage every little thing. You have to set things up in advance and let them put their own personal touch on it. You should have meetings before you start any practice. You can always make adjustments even when you are in the middle of the season. Decide in advance what you want to run and who is in charge of what positions and different aspects of the team, like play calling on offense and defense. Once you are satisfied they know what you want, then leave them alone, let them do their thing. If you have a problem then discuss it after practice or before you start the next one. If it is something that needs attention right away, go off to one side or out of earshot of the team to make your point. Never, never, never, never, do I have to continue? Never correct or discipline a coach in front of players. If you have to do that you need to let him go and find someone who can fit into the program a little better. While we are on the subject of correcting and disciplining let's look at the rest of the team.

Members of the team are just that, a team. What's good for one is good for all. Sure there may be an occasion to take action on one player but that is a case-by-case call, for the most part try to build team togetherness in everything you do. I will try to build on this concept a little more in future chapters but I want to focus on assistant coaches, they are a vital part of coaching. You cannot do it all yourself so learning to handle assistants is very important. You want them to feel like their point of view is valued and appreciated but the final decision is always the head coach's. Learn to listen and repeat back what they said, then take the time to respond to what they said even if you don't agree. Don't just say "No that will not work." Let them hear from you why you want to go in a different direction. If you cut them off all the time you will kill their creativity and shut down the communication lines that are valuable in building a team not just a team of players but a team of coaches.

I was in a game one time and my son came out of the stands to tell me something he saw on the field. He felt that this would make a play I was trying to run work better. I shut him down and sent him back to the stands. He didn't go back to the stands but went to my other son who was on the sideline helping me coach. A few moments later they came back and cornered me and made me listen. I saw the wisdom in their words and made the correction to the play. We ran it again and about ten seconds later, we had six more points. In the past I let my sons voice their opinions on everything and at first I thought it came back to bite me. Then I realized I was not living my own advice. If I would have shut them down as kids growing up, he would have never come out of the stands to help me. He would have just said to himself, "Oh he won't listen to me, just forget it." It's true in the past they may have had some screwball ideas but that does not mean they can't come up with something great. Listen to your coaches, listen to your players, you don't have to do what they say, remember you are still the King.

Let's get started

I don't care what offense you want to run but there are a few basics that have become standard in the football world. One would be the position names and numbering system. There may be some teams with little changes to the names of positions but for the most part the numbering is universal throughout football. (See example below.)

This first diagram shows the names of the positions, there will always be a slight variation between coaches but if you know the basics you will be able to translate them into your own language.

Slot Right

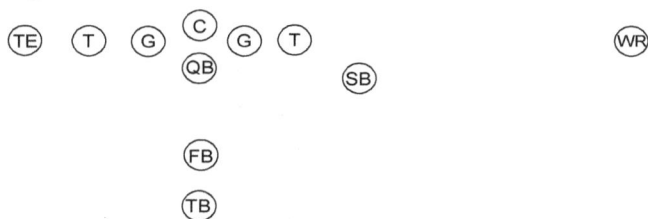

TE	Tight End		
T	Tackle	SB	Slot Back, Wing
G	Guard	QB	Quarterback
C	Center	FB	Fullback, 3 Back
WR	Wide Receiver, Split End	TB	Tailback, 2 Back

Numbering

On the right side of the line they will be even numbers starting with "zero", on the right side of the center. Then moving right they will increase by two. The two hole, four, six and eight, the eight is also used to signify the sweep.

On the left side they are odd numbers, starting with one which is on the left side of the center. Then moving left they go - three, five, seven, and nine also used as the sweep number in some offenses.

Now the backs' numbers are set up by position starting with the quarterback as one, then the tailback being two and the fullback would be three. The slot back is most of the time four and that is your backfield. The wide receiver is called the wide receiver or wide out, and is most of the time split out wide on one side of the formation or the other. The tight end is the man who lines up on the line of scrimmage with the rest of the linemen, but has to be on the end with no one to his outside in order to be eligible to receive a pass. You can have an eligible receiver on his outside but they must not be on the line. If they are, then the tight end becomes ineligible.

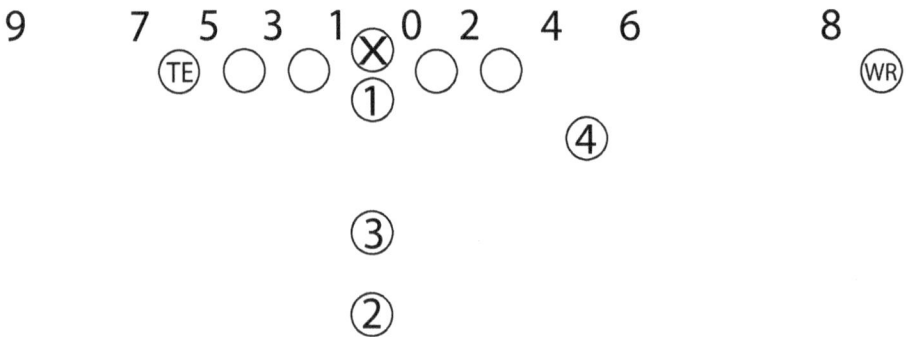

Spacing

A quick word about spacing. It is the distance between the players on the line of scrimmage and the spacing of the backfield. This is as diverse as there are coaches. I put one foot between the linemen and have them back off the center stance about a foot as well. The slot back is about a yard back and over. On the wing I will bring the four back in tighter. The backfield will start with the quarterback under center and the three back two to three yards behind him. The two back is one to two feet behind the three back. The wide receiver is in from the sideline about five to seven yards. That will also go for the tight end if we are in a spread. If I know I want to run a sideline pattern in a game I will bring the four back in more to allow room for the pattern. That is the basic rule but you will have to adjust it to the age, size and speed of your team.

Formations

There are as many formations as there are programs but you can only use a few so as you see the ones you like whether in this book or anywhere you happen to be, make a note of them and add them to the workbook. Most of the formations can be flipped over to make them a new line up. The slot right can be flipped to be a slot left and so on.

Wing right
The wing right starts out with three linemen including the tight end on the left side of the center. They are in a three-point stance with about twelve inches space in between the feet of the player next to him and they are left of the center. On the right side you have three linemen as well with one being the wide receiver, however most teams will take out the wide receiver and bring in an additional tight end and they are also in a three-point stance. The slot back in this formation is called the wing, he will be in tight and back off the line making both tight ends eligible. I will split the backfield, with the two back over the two hole and the three back over the three hole. The two backs will be two to three yards back depending on their speed, size, age and ability. This formation will give you a lot

more power on the line. I use the wing a lot on short yardage situations including goal line and where I want to bring everybody in close because I feel I have a bigger and stronger team. If that doesn't turn out the way I planned, I will keep them in tight and try to use speed to the outside. Still if that proves unsuccessful then trickery is my next plan of attack.

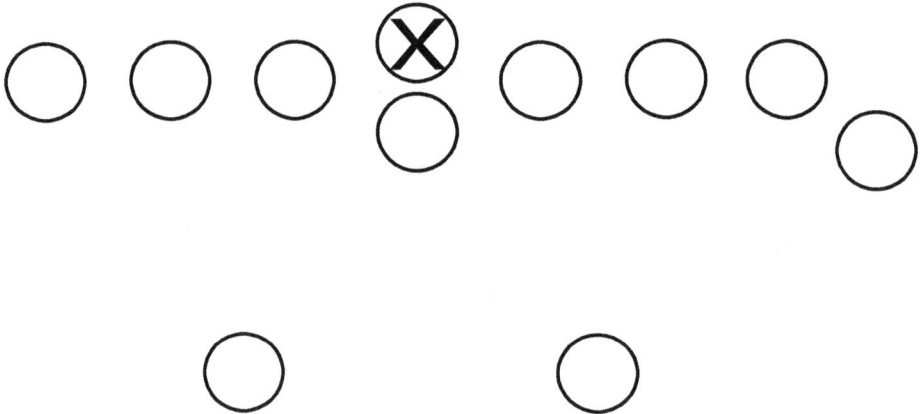

Spread right

The spread is a general term depending on the coach. There are a lot of spread formations and even a few spread offenses. The one I use is for a particular set of plays I like to run. Some spread formations have less people in the backfield and maybe overload one side with receivers. Some have no backfield. I will just show you one but this is a great example of "Do what works for you." I go into a spread right by splitting my tight end out to the left side five to seven yards from the sideline and on the line of scrimmage. I move my slot back or wing back depending on what you want to call him but for now we can call him the four back. I put him out wide to the right side with the wide receiver and have him just inside and back off the line of scrimmage, two to three yards. The backs are split with the two back over the two hole and the three back over the three hole. With this formation I am just trying to weaken the middle or pass the ball.

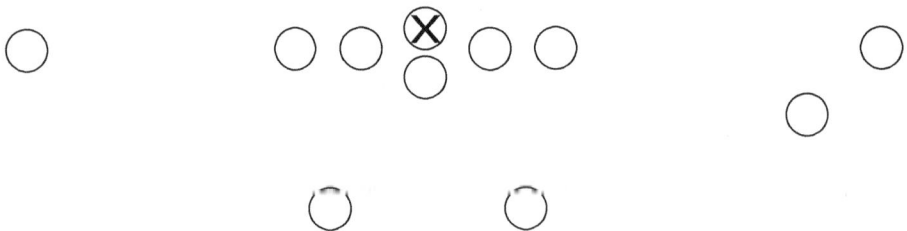

Slot right

The slot right is the formation I use most of the time; it is set up with three linemen on the left side of the center and two on the right. The center is over the ball with one hand on the ball and one on the ground; the other linemen including the tight end are set back about one foot off the line of scrimmage. They are in a three-point stance and set about one foot apart. The slot back is about one yard back and one yard to the right of the right tackle. The wide receiver is split out about five to seven yards from the sideline. The quarterback is under center with the full back or three back one and a half to two yards behind the quarterback. The tailback or two back is one half yards behind the full back. This is where you start, then you make the adjustments according to their size, speed and ability.

The slot for me is the perfect formation. It gives me the ability to run to both sides and throw the ball without having to make a lot of adjustments to the formation. In addition to that the defense can't get a lot of clues as to what I'm going to do next because I start most of my plays from the same formation.

I will use the slot formation with an "I" backfield, with much the same concept as the true option, disguising what I'm doing behind the same line up each time. The quarterbacks don't have to make a lot of reads on the defense, I do that for them by picking up on the defenses tendencies and calling the play that will take advantage of that tendency. I will get into that more in the future chapters.

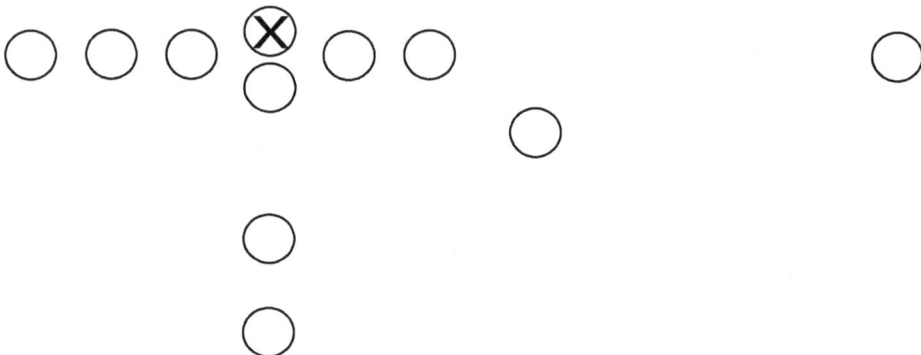

Power "I"

The power "I" is just an even formation with the slot back or wing back in the backfield with the two running backs to allow you a lot of power inside.

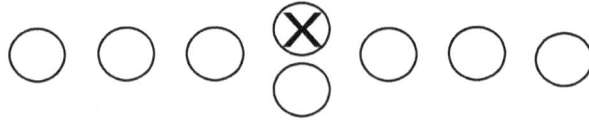

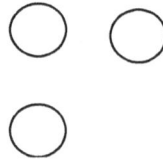

Veer

The veer is not only a formation it is also an offense, much like a triple option. It gives you power to both sides equally.

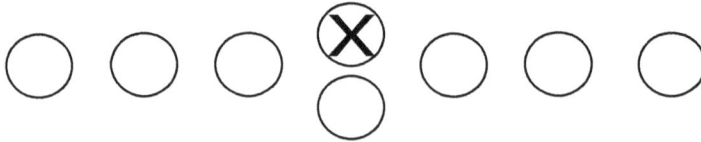

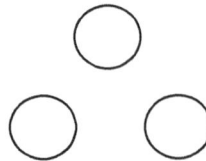

Spread, Trips Right

With this alignment you put a lot of your receivers to one side of the formation flooding that side and putting a lot of pressure on their zone pass defense.

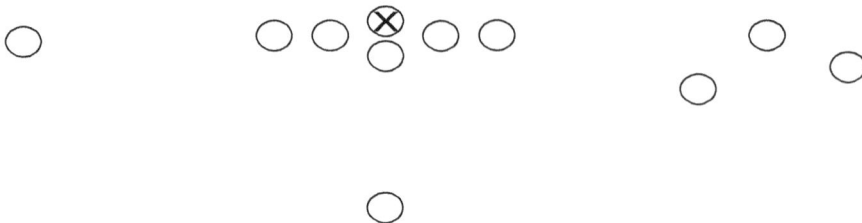

Pass Patterns

Pass patterns have a number of different names depending on what the coaches want to call them. It really doesn't matter as long as everyone on your team uses the same name. I put together a sheet of paper to give to every player so that there is no confusion within the team. Look over these few patterns and use what ones you like, but don't feel like you have to stick to mine, there are a lot of patterns to choose from, these are just to get started. You may also just want to change them a little to fit what you are doing.

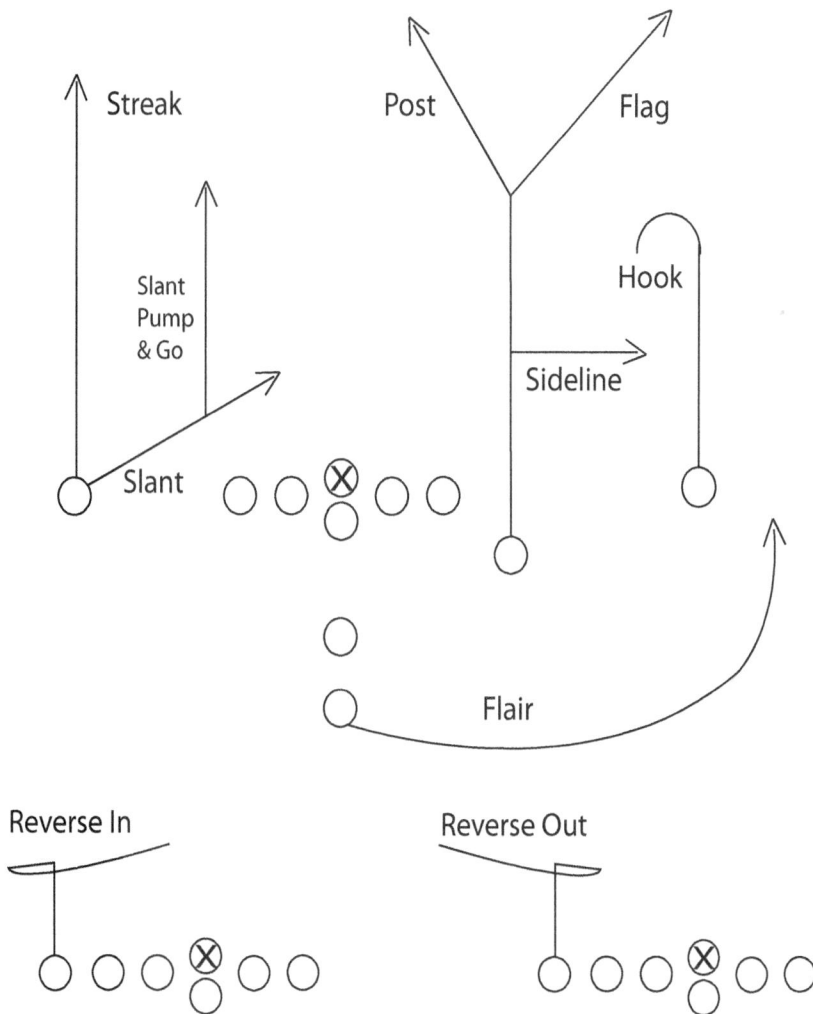

Pump and go

As you look over the pass patterns you will see that I include one pump and go route. They can be run with almost any short pattern you just have to add that to the end of the route or pattern. I put it on the slant route but there are some keys to this play that I will go over in later chapters that are very important in order for the pump and go to work.

Now that we've gone over a few formations and spacing, I hope that gives you a much better picture on where and how you should line them up. There are a lot of formations out there but I have found that I can do everything I need to do with just three. The three I use allow me to run my offense and all the plays I need to win without getting too complicated. However, just because I only use three formations, that doesn't mean you have to. Don't think you have to have a lot of different formations to get the job done. You don't and you don't want to lug around a heavy toolbox full of tools you don't need. Travel light but travel smart. (More on that later.)

Play Calling

Now that you have the numbering system and some basic formations you need to be able to call a play using a simple plan that allows you to make it clear and easy to understand. The way I do it seems to work and I never have a player say to me I didn't understand the call.

Let's just start with some simple calls like thirty-three, that is the three back to the three hole, twenty-four is the two back to the four hole. Twenty-nine is a sweep to the left or the nine-hole which is really not a hole as much as it is an end run. Same as the twenty-eight it is a sweep to the right side of the formation.

I start with a slot right formation. This will always be the same unless I say different. That goes for the backfield as well. Slot right means the formation is a slot right and the backs set up in an "I", the backs don't have to think about it. Unless I say split they are always in an "I" back-field.

Slot right twenty-four is run just like it sounds with an "I" backfield. If I want to change it I would just say. Slot right split twenty-two dive. Then the backs would split with the two back over the two hole and the three back over the three hole. If I wanted the backfield to cross first, I would say slot right split twenty-two cross. The three back will line up over the two hole and the two back over the three hole. Then at the snap of the ball the three back will go first to the three hole and the two back will take a step to the three side then go to the two hole. The quarterback will open to the three side then hand the ball back to the two back.

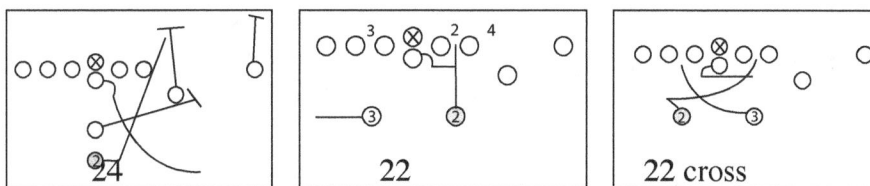

I very rarely split the backs but if you are going to run a quick pitch in your offense you need to split the backs or they will not be able to get outside the defensive ends before they get the ball. Which will leave you with a problem, if that is the only play you run from the split backfield you may be giving it away, so you will have to have at least a couple of plays using the split back field to keep them guessing. It is always a good idea to have run plays and pass plays from the same formation.

Calling a pass play

If I want to run a pass play I will just add the word pass to the call. Slot right **pass** twenty-four. This would not change the formation just a few assignments. If I want a particular player to get the ball other than the way we usually run it I can add that to the call as well. Slot right, pass twenty-four tight end **streak**, or slot back **post**. The last part of the call is where the ball is going.

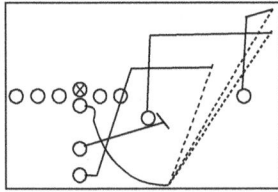

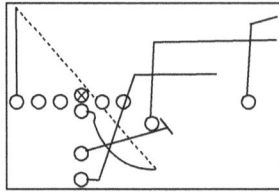

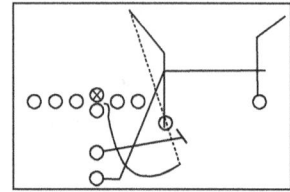

| Pass 24 | Pass 24 TE streak | Pass 24 SB post |

I can call almost any play from almost any formation, but some plays take a particular formation to work. One such play is the **tight-end slant**. You can't run it from a slot formation it has to be run from a spread. I don't have to say split on this formation for the backs because on the spread that will be their normal set position. So to call this play I would just say **spread right tight-end slant**. This play is so fast you don't need a lot of play action in the backfield. That is why there was no call for the backfield and no pass in the call. The call tells the story, the only player getting the call is the tight-end and the only way he can get the ball on a slant pattern is if the quarterback throws it to him. I can change the pass pattern by simple changing the call at the end of the play. Spread right tight-end post. Now he runs a **post** instead of the slant.

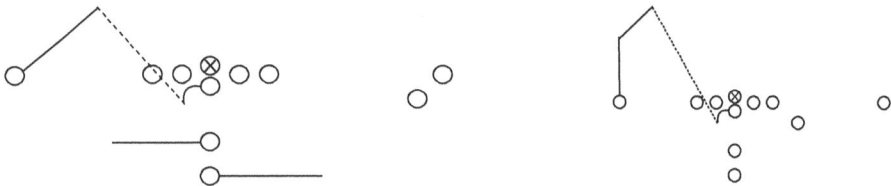

If you wanted to add a particular blocking scheme just put it in. Spread right **fire**, tight-end slant. Fire could mean fire out to the linemen or protect which could mean pass block. Spread right, **right side protect**, tight-end slant.

If there is more than one pattern called or more than one action for the receivers the last part of the call is where I want the ball to go. Spread right wide receiver **slant slot back post**. I want everything to stay the same but the slot back that will change his assignment from a block downfield to a post pattern with him being the number one receiver. The last command is the play.

The **pass thirty-three tight-end delay** is not a thirty-three but a tight end delay. Later in the season I don't even have to say pass first on this play because the last command is the tight end delay. Thirty-three tight end delay, and by next year if I have a lot of the same kids it becomes just a tight end delay.

By using a simple sequence of play calling I can make changes in a play without having everybody learn something new. If I run a wide receiver slant and I see they have no safety or if the safety is stepping up on the slant, I can change it to a **wide receiver slant slot back post**. The only player doing something different is the slot back. Now I have the slot back slip the block on the linebacker and have him do a post. As long as I teach them the basics on pass route running on each pattern it is easy to build on a play even during a game.

There are a lot more very important keys to making these and other plays like it work, but I will get into that in later chapters. For now let's stay on play calling and setting up your offense.

I try to keep it as simple as I can; adding too much to a play or play calling will invite misunderstanding and end in a blown play. Don't make it more than it has to be. In my years of being a head coach I had one losing season and I never pass blocked and with the exceptions of a few trick plays only three offensive formations. I'm not saying you have to only have three formations. Just because that worked for me it doesn't mean it will work for you. The only thing I can say with certainty is "*KISS - Keep It Simple Stupid*".

Offensive Plays

Formations are meaningless until you have an offense to use them with, so let's talk some more about offense. I will use my own for now and you can make changes to it or try another. But before you can change something you first have to have something.

I start out with slot right twenty-four because I run a lot of plays off of it. This play has to run smooth before I can move on, or I can't run the rest of my offense.

Slot right twenty-four

Let's start with the slot right formation, the linemen fire out to the man over or first inside. That means that he takes the man over him or if there is no one over him then the one who is to his inside. These blocking assignments stay the same on every play that starts out like a twenty-four which is a lot of them. Even if it's a pass they still fire out as if it were a run. As you may have seen from previous chapters the quarterback opens on the right side then starts back to the tailback or two back. We want to get the ball to the tailback as far back in the backfield as we can. The tailback takes his first step to the right, keeping his shoulders square to the line of scrimmage then runs to the four hole. The full back or three back, takes a line to the defensive end and kicks him out. The slot back takes the linebacker out and that is the block the tailback will key off of. The offensive-guard and tackle will double on the defensive guard or tackle, depending on who is there. If they are both there, they take the man over them. The quarterback continues on the same rounded arch to the outside of the play. The defensive end will usually take himself out of the play. If he doesn't then I call a slot right twenty-four quarterback keeper.

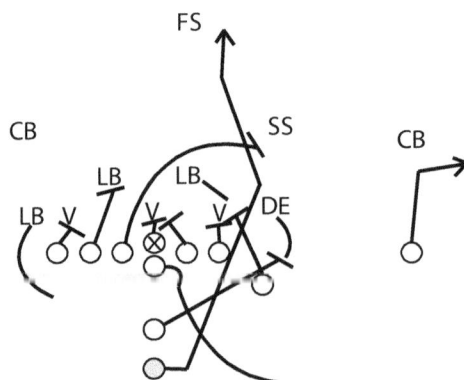

Slot right twenty-four quarterback keeper

Here the quarterback fakes the twenty-four and keeps the ball and continues with an arching pattern around the end like a quarterback sweep. The quarterback does not have to read any defensive formations or players he is just running the play that I called. The three back will block the defensive end but this time he will try to hook him instead of kicking him out. The rest of the play will stay the same.

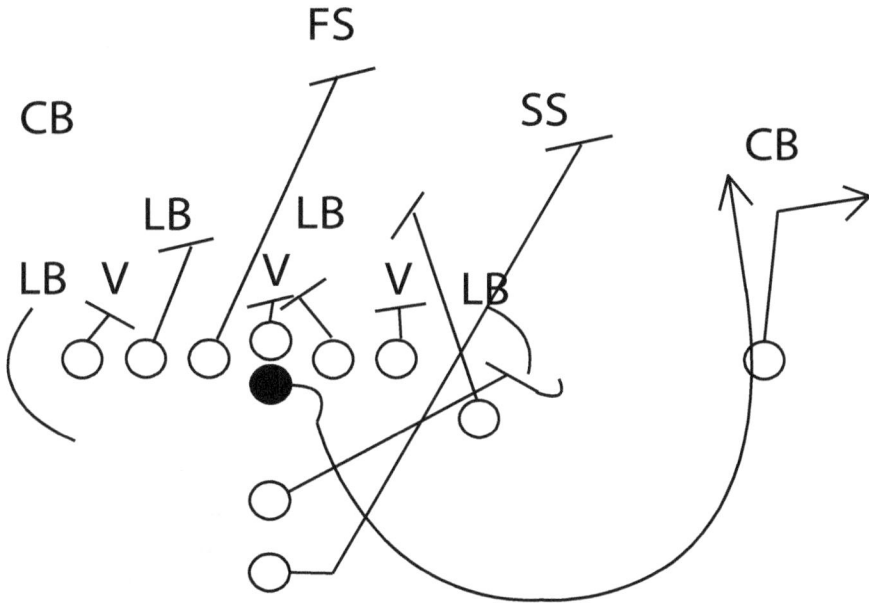

Slot right pass twenty-four

The pass twenty-four, says pass in it but I like to think of it as a run first, pass second that is why it is in the running section, however I will put it in the passing section as well.

This play like most plays starts out like a twenty-four, the linemen do the same block as the twenty-four but the backfield will change their assignments a little. The full back will have the same man but will try to hook him instead of kicking him out. The tailback will go for the same linebacker that before tried to stop him, but this time he hits him then slides off the block and goes on a five-yard sideline pattern. The slot back will do a seven to nine yard sideline pattern and the wide receiver will do a fifteen-yard flag. The quarterback will have to read on this play. He can throw it to one of the open receivers or run the ball. I always say run first, green means go defender means throw. Green being the grass, if he sees a lot of grass then I want him to take off and get as many yards as he can. I want the other team to start thinking about the quarterback and his ability to run.

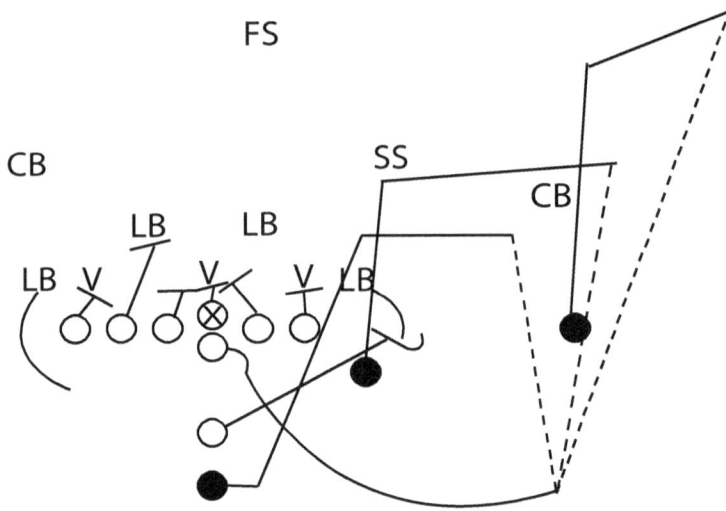

Slot right thirty-four

Everything is the same as the twenty-four except the tailback and the full back change assignments. Now the three back gets the ball and the two back goes for the defensive end. This is a much quicker play to the four hole and if they are coming hard on the play and you ran the twenty-four a few times they will not see the three back go thru the hole until they see the ball not in the two backs' hands.

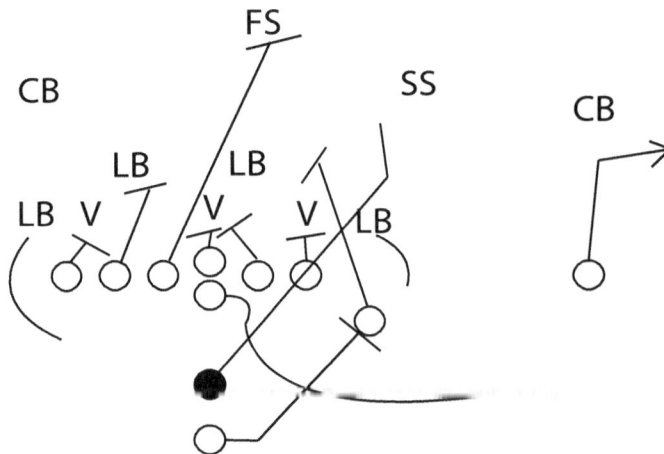

Slot right twenty-three cross

Everything is the same as the twenty-four except for the tailback and the linemen on the three side. The backs stay in an "I" formation because I didn't say split and I don't want the defense to know what I'm about to run. The tailback will start with the same step to his right like a twenty-four keeping his shoulders square to the line of scrimmage then cuts back to the three hole. The linemen will let the defense take a step to the four hole then seal up the left side for the cutback. You must run the twenty-four a few times first before you run this one.

FS

CB   SS

Too late

LB ---- LB ---

CB

LB V   V   V LB

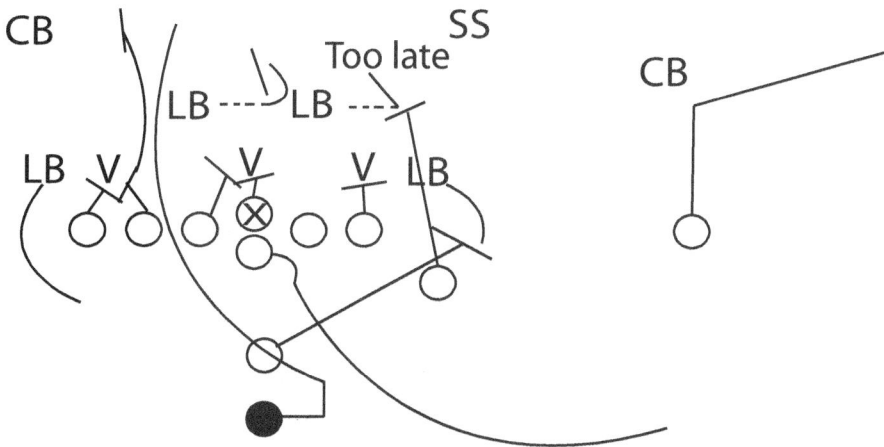

Slot right forty-seven reverse

This play starts out just like a twenty-four and up until the ball goes the other way you want it to remain that way. Everybody does the same thing as a twenty-four except the slot back and maybe the left guard. (This is the play I mentioned earlier where my son came out of the stands to add the left guard.) The slot back has to take a step or two to the right before he turns around and heads in the opposite direction. The quarterback fakes it to the two back then takes a few steps as if he is running the quarter-back keeper and just a few steps maybe two or three. Then as the slot back comes by, he hands it to him. I will make the slot back do a loop to the right and a yard or two deeper into the backfield first before he comes back the other way. I want him to be going towards the line of scrimmage at an angle as he gets the ball. Not a big angle but enough to make it easy on the turn up field. You will have to work with the timing on this play to get it to run smooth. This is a faster reverse than most of the reverses you see on TV so don't be surprised when you first try to run it.

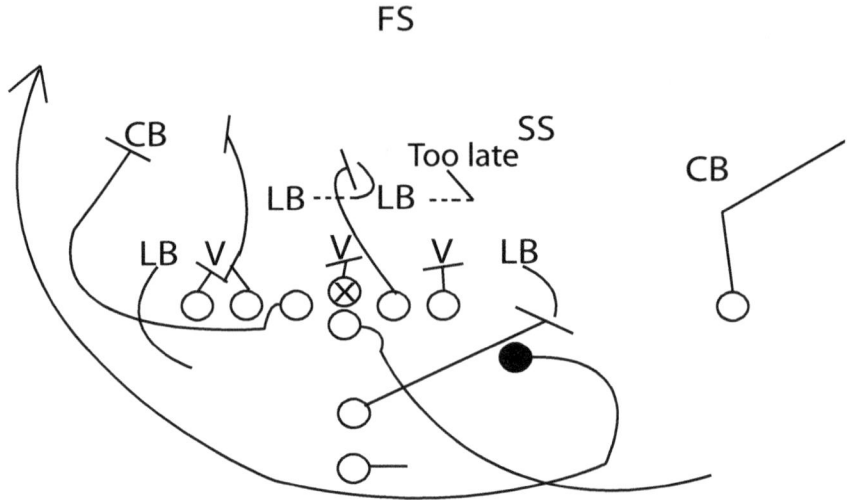

When you run the reverse with the slot back rather than the wide receiver it is hard for the defense to see it coming. When you run it with the wide receiver the defensive backs will see the wide receiver start back the other way and start yelling reverse. With the slot back they will not see him loop back because they are going for the two back on the fake twenty-four, even the defensive end will crash down on the twenty-four. I ran it a lot without the pulling guard and it worked ok so you can try it both ways and see what works for you.

Slot right split thirty-three

I add the split backfield to the play, you can have them line up that way out of the huddle, or they can split on the count like, ready, set, hut, split on ready. The quarterback opens to the three side, this is a quick play and there is no time to reverse out for the quarterback, you want the three back to hit the hole as fast as he can. The blocking is, man over or first inside or if there is no man over him on the line he could go after the linebacker. The quarterback will continue out to the tight end and block him. The tailback goes in the opposite direction. That is a general rule on all plays. If you are not getting the ball and you have no call in the huddle, then go the opposite way as the play.

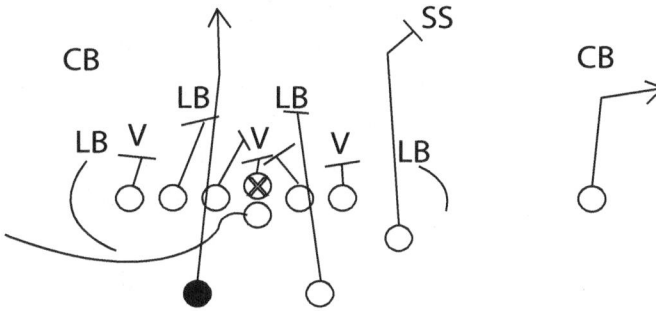

Slot right split twenty-nine quick pitch

This is also a very quick play and has very important details to running it right. I never run this to a side where there is a receiver split wide like in a spread formation. You can run this from a slot but only to the side without the wide receiver or slot back. The quarterback must reverse out to the even side, then make the pitch that is the longest he will ever toss. (Check the toss on the DVD, it can be done.) It will have to be fast and hard. The tailback runs to the left as fast as he can. He must not worry about the toss that is the quarterback's job. The two back will get the ball outside the offensive tackle, the further the better. (I would like to see him get the ball outside the tight end if the quarterback can do it.) The two backs' job is to get as much speed to the outside before he makes his round house turn downfield. I use the two back most of the time but you can do either one as long as you put him on the side with the call if not it is just a sweep.

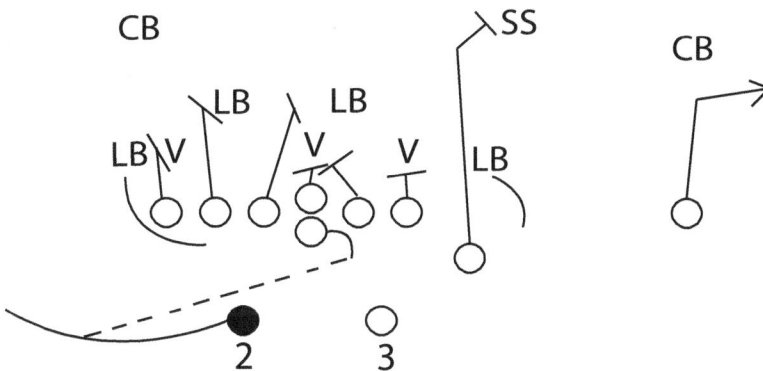

Slot right twenty-four lead

The lead is just a small adjustment to the blocking for the full back. Instead of blocking the defensive end he will go thru the hole and hit the linebacker. The only other thing that might change is the slot back if the defensive end goes out wide and takes himself out of the play, the slot back takes his normal guy the linebacker. If the defensive end crashes down on the play then he takes the defensive end. (If the defensive end is crashing and disrupting this play, that is a very good thing and I will show you later what to do about that.) The twenty-three lead is the same just on the other side but there is no slot back to get the end, however there is another man on the line so the defensive end is further away from the play. The lead tells the full back to go thru the hole first to block.

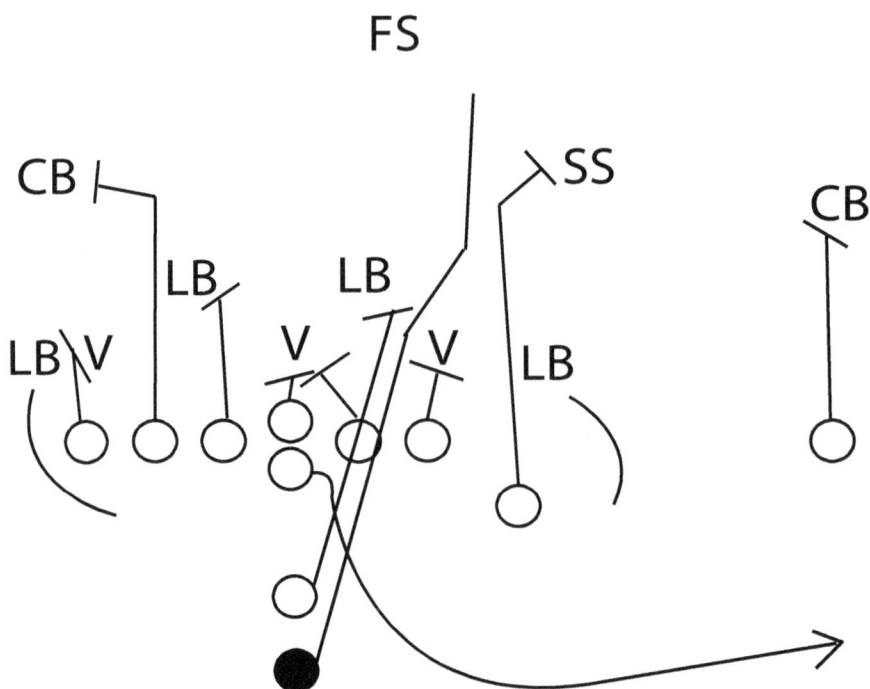

FS

CB   SS   CB

LB   LB   LB   LB   LB

Slot right quarterback one step draw

The quarterback takes one step back and holds the ball up like a pass, then brings it down and runs like heck. I mean fast and straight up the field. You can have the linemen stand up as to simulate a pass blocking stance then just let the defensive linemen go past them. I just use the same block as the rest of the plays (fire out).

This is a very quick play and it is designed to take advantage of blitzing linebackers and an aggressive defensive line, especially the nose guard. The quarterback will key off of him and go whatever way he's not. If the nose guard is slanting to the slot side then the quarterback will go slightly left just off the block of the center, same if he is slanting left then the quarterback goes right.

There is also a drop back draw where the quarterback will drop all the way into the pocket before he takes off. You can give the quarterback the number of steps you want him to take before he goes or just let him decide for himself if you think he can handle it.

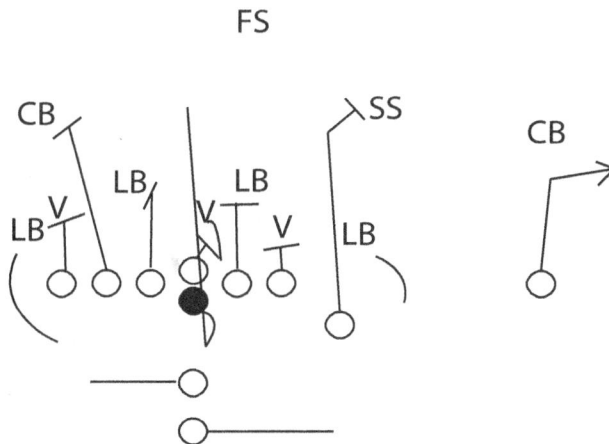

Slot right twenty-eight power and super power

This is just a sweep with a pulling guard or two pulling guards. Power is one guard and super power is two guards. That is really all there is to this play. The full back leads the play and the rest is as they say, football. You can run it either way and with either back. Just change the call to a twenty-nine or a thirty-nine or twenty-eight or thirty-eight. You can also run this from a split backfield if you want to get the lead block (full back) a head start.

31

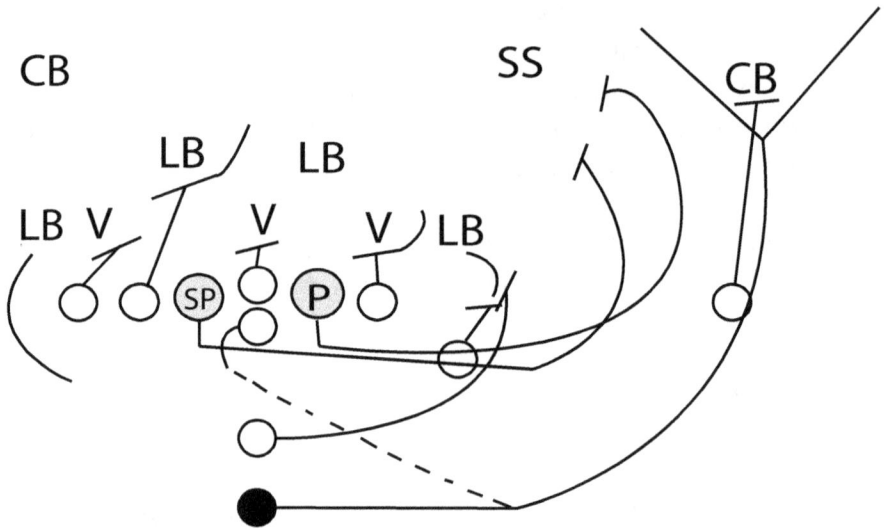

Now if you haven't already started to put your plays down in the workbook you should do it now and as you go along in this book you can add and/or take out plays you like or don't like until you have a number of plays to start with. Then you can keep building as we go along.

In a later chapter I will put you in a game like situation and go through a sequence of plays to show you how to use these plays in order to take advantage of the defense and what they might be doing or not doing, but for now just think of them as tools you will need later.

Passing

Passing is fun and sometimes more dramatic. The when and where is also in later chapters, but for now I want you to think of it as just another tool for the job. Like with all tools you want to keep them sharp and ready to use when the situation calls for it. That is a hit on teaching the basics and with passing you don't want your tools to get rusty, you want them sharp and ready to use at all times. That's what you do in practice. Remember, practice does not make perfect but "perfect practice makes perfect". I will show you in later chapters what I think a perfect practice looks like and why.

Now a word or many on the different kinds of passes you can teach and use. One is the low and hard pass. (You will want to see the DVD to see what I'm talking about.) When thrown correctly the ball looks like it is on a string, I use this one for the tight end slant.

Two, is the traditional pass that looks the prettiest and has a nice arch with a perfectly spinning spiral.

Three, is the loop pass that doesn't have to look pretty or spin nice it's just a little toss that drops into a space like over the linemen and in front of the defensive backs.

The last is what I call anyway you can. I don't care what it looks like or how you throw it, as long as it gets to the right place at the right time.

Slot right pass twenty-four

I use this play as a run as well, that is why you have seen it in the running section, but now I want to elaborate more on the passing side of this play. First of all I want this play to look as much like a twenty-four as possible right up to the point where it turns into a pass play. To everyone but the wide receiver, slot back and the tailback it will be a twenty-four that way the linebackers and ends will try to get the tailback and not have time to get back into pass coverage.

The quarterback will run the play like a twenty-four but will keep the ball and continue to the outside, at this point he can choose to pass the ball or keep it. I will tell him to always run first, pass second; I want the defensive backs and linebackers to be thinking that the quarterback can run. That way they have to decide whether or not they want to stay back in coverage or rush the passer, which will help spread them out and give more room for the quarterback to move.

The wide receiver will run a fifteen-yard flag while the slot back and tail-back will run a sideline pattern. The slot back is about ten-yards deep and the tailback about two to five. If the linebacker goes for the fake that will just leave two defensive backs on three receivers. If all the receivers are covered then have the quarterback run the ball and get as many yards as possible, this will help later on in the game.

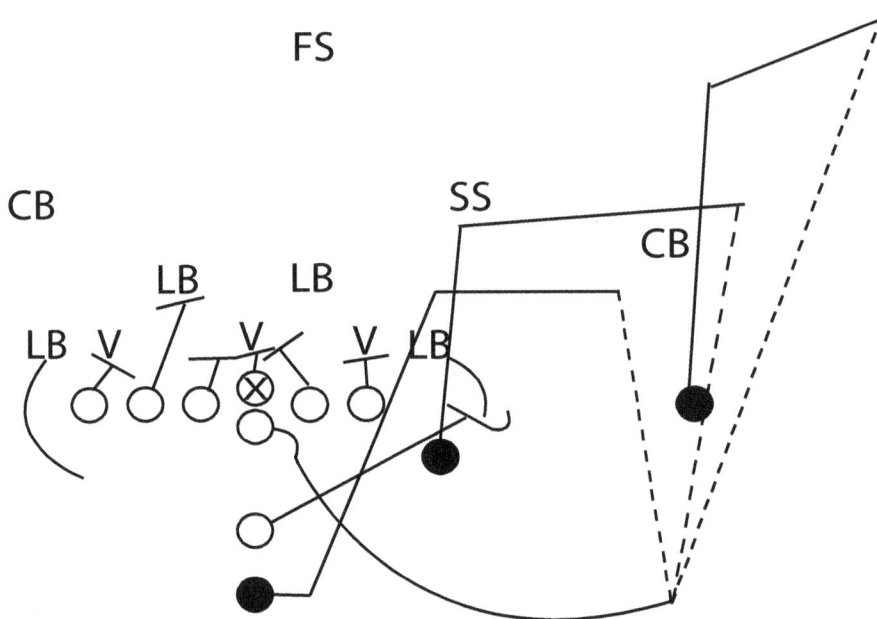

Slot right pass twenty-four tight end post
This play is the same as a pass twenty-four with just one adjustment to the tight ends' pattern. This time he will run a post pattern, hopefully you ran the basic pass twenty-four and you saw the free safety going hard to your wide receivers flag pattern. When he does that it leaves the corner back one-on-one with the tight end. Sometimes you will want to put in a faster tight end or sneak in a wide receiver to run this pattern.

On this play the quarterback will have little time to stop and throw the ball back against the grain. I will have him try to take a deeper track so that he will be running forward when he has to release the ball.

Slot right pass twenty-four slot back streak

By now you must have noticed that almost all of the plays start out as a twenty-four. By now you may have also noticed that it is very easy to change the play with just a few words added to the call. Just add slot back streak to the call and now the slot back is the only player who changes his assignment, now he runs a new pass route. The quarterback will start out with the twenty-four and stop just after the tailback passes him. He will set his feet and make the throw. He has to get the ball to the receiver just after he clears the linebackers and before he gets to the safety. It is not a long pass maybe five to seven yards. You want to look for the strong safety or whoever is over the slot back. When they move him up, or over in a vain attempt to stop the twenty-four and pass twenty-four that is when you want to run this play.

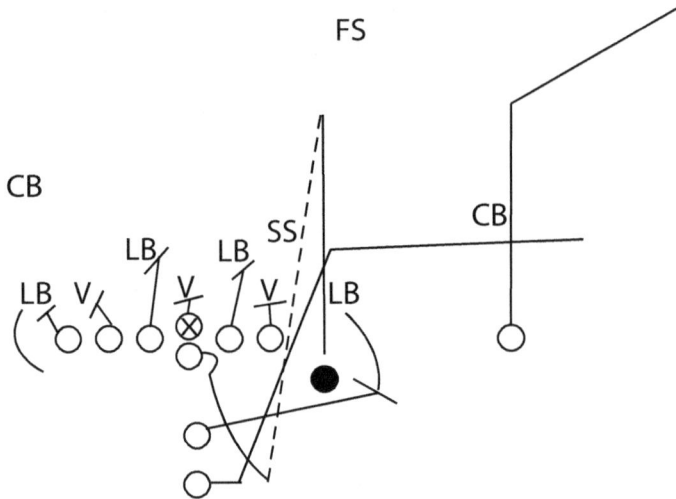

Slot right pass twenty-four tight end quick streak

The keys to this play, as to when and how to run it, are when the linebackers are up close and moving forward on the snap of the ball, the other is that it is quicker than most of the twenty-four passes. The quarterback will not wait for the tailback to pass him before he turns and passes the ball to the tight end. This is also a loop pass over the heads of the defenders, it doesn't have to be pretty it just has to be on time. The other thing to look for on this play is the safety; for the most part he will be over the slot back on the other side of the defensive formation and way out of the play, but be sure. Side note, I might run this play first before I ran the twenty-nine quick pitch to bring the defensive back in closer.

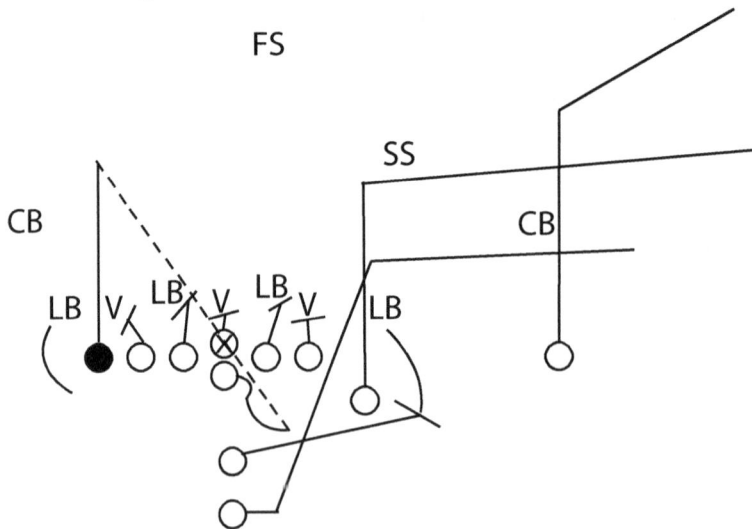

Slot right pass twenty-four bootleg tight end wiggle

The quarterback keeps the ball and rolls out to the back side of the play, at this point he can run or pass, you know I always say run first pass second. The tight end will run a very short pass route then loop back for the block. Then release the block and do a sideline pattern. If the defensive back comes up after the quarterback then he will throw the pass to the tight end, if the defensive back stays back in coverage then the quarterback will run.

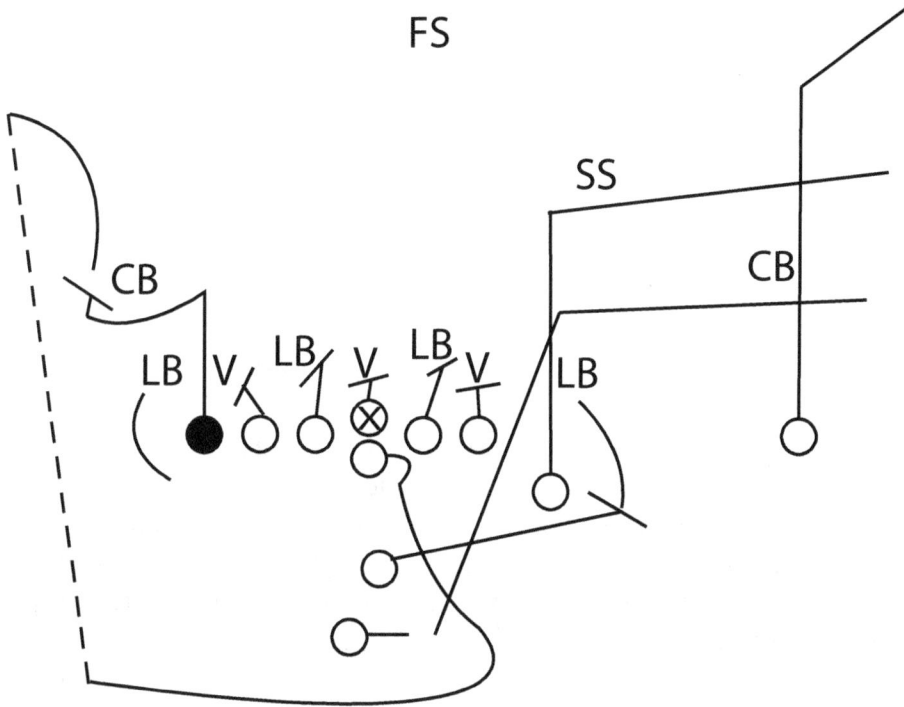

FS

SS

CB

CB

LB   V   LB   V   LB   V   LB

Slot right pass twenty-four tight end reverse in

The tight end will do a short sideline route to the left or outside, then reverse his direction and go across the field to the right. The quarterback will stop about half way on the sprint out route and throw back to the tight end. The linebackers should be going hard to the right if you ran the twenty-four enough times prior to this play.

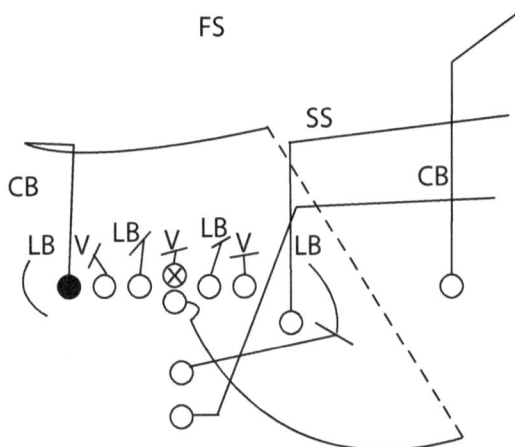

Slot right pass twenty-four tight-end scrape

On this play the scrape pattern is a long route to run for the tight end and it takes time to develop. So, the quarterback will try to get deeper on his sprint out route to allow more time for the tight end to come out of the pack to receive the ball. The two receivers on the right side run deep routes usually a flag and/or a post. I like the post it gives the tight end more space to run up the sideline. Now that the two receivers on the slot side have cleared out the safety and the defensive backs there should be a large gap in the coverage on that side. The tight end starts his route at about five yards or I tell him to get behind the linebackers, then he angles slightly downfield to take advantage of the vacating defensive back and safety. This pattern starts on the left and carries all the way across to the right side where he will receive the ball. It is important that the tight end gets behind the linebackers so they don't follow him to the other side. The quarterback fakes to the two back to help keep the linebackers in tight so the tight end has no trouble getting behind them.

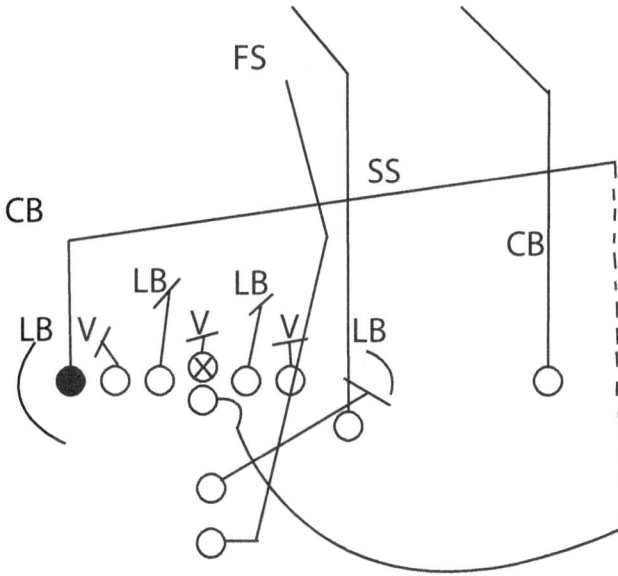

Spread right wide receiver slant

I don't say pass in the call because there is only one thing happening and no time for any tricky blocking or a fake to the backs. The same will go for all the quick passes unless I call a backfield action they will go the opposite way as the play or ball. This is a different formation and a fast play. There is no call for the backfield the full back will go left to block the defensive end as the two back goes left as well. The quarterback stands up and delivers the ball low and hard as quickly as he can. The slot back runs straight and fast to get out of the way and to get the safety out of the play. The linemen fire out low and hard to keep the defensive linemen in tight and the linebackers coming forward.

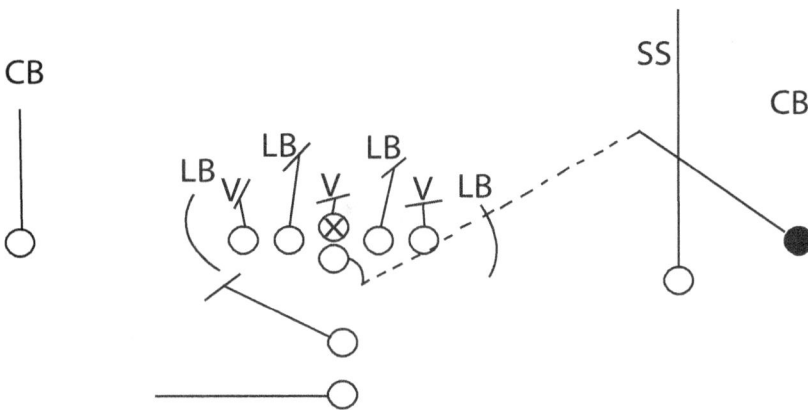

Spread right tight end slant

The same play as the wide receiver slant but to the other side. Now you don't have the slot back to get out of the way and the safety is on the other side. The play is even quicker if you can convince the quarterback to just stand and throw the ball. It doesn't have to be a pretty pass it just has to get there fast and low. The backs just go to the right this time and the linemen fire out low and hard to keep the defensive linemen and the linebackers coming forward.

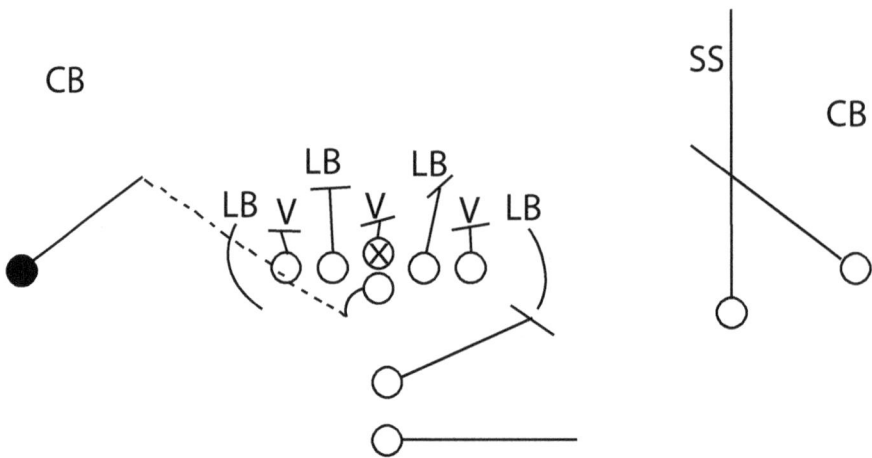

Spread right tight end slant pump and go

This is the same play as the tight end slant but with one very big change. The tight end will run a slant and then a streak. The timing and the details on this play are of the utmost importance. One, the tight end takes three steps on the slant pattern, the three steps are. Right, left, right. On the last right step he plants his foot and turns up field also on the third step he looks at the quarterback, he also must put his hands up to simulate the catching motion The quarterback must fake and pass the ball all in one motion. One, two, the ball's away. Yes it's that fast and yes everybody tells me it can't be done, until I show them a ten-year old doing it, then they say, "Oh? Ok." (You must see the DVD on this one, I am afraid I will not be able to tell the story well enough for you to see how the little things make this play work.) An important side note is you can only run this play once or twice in a game so make sure you run it right and at the right time because it is a long play and/or a touchdown.

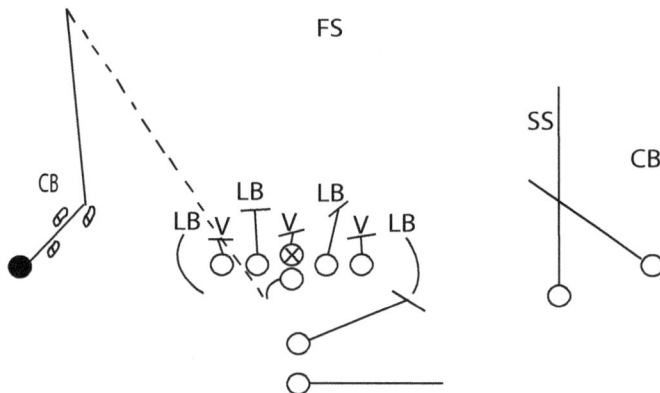

Slot right tailback flair

The quarterback takes a five to seven step drop and throws the ball to the tailback on the flair route. The slot back runs a five to seven yard hook to keep the linebacker inside, and the wide receiver runs a post or flag to clear out the corner back and safety. The quarterback should look off the defense by watching the slot back until he is ready to throw the flair. The slot back can make a block on the linebacker before the pass as long as the pass is behind the line of scrimmage.

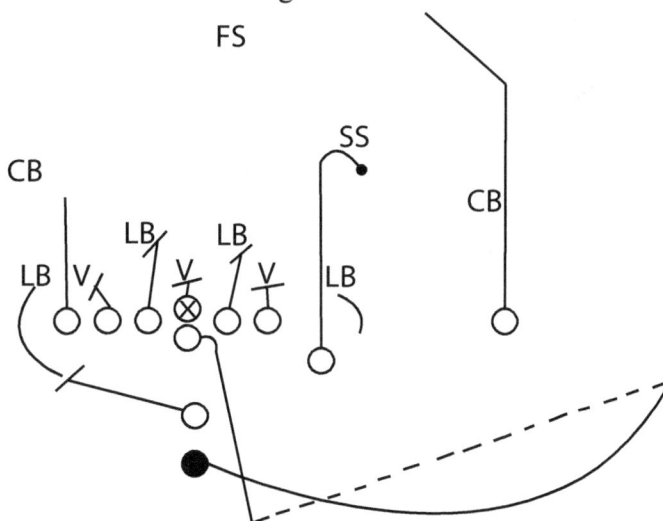

Slot right pass thirty-three tight end delay

The keys to this play are many and very important, some have to do with the mechanics of the play as well as the down and distance. Let's start with the quarterback, he will take a large step left and into the backfield.

The three back will run to the three hole and act like he's getting the ball. The quarterback will put the ball in the belly of the three back and ride that for as long as he can by taking his right foot and stepping forward towards the three hole. The quarterback rides the three back as far into the line as he can, then will pull the ball out of the belly of the full back, take a step back and throw the ball to the tight end. The tight end will first put a block on the defensive end, then slips the block and runs directly to the sideline, no more than one to two yards deep. He must make the block first and he must go towards the sideline. Any deeper and the linebacker and defensive back will follow him. If the tight end doesn't hit the defensive end first, then the linebacker and defensive back will follow him. If the quarterback doesn't put the ball in the belly of the full back and ride it to the line of scrimmage, the linebacker and defensive back will follow the tight end. If the tailback doesn't go right then the right side linebacker will follow the tight end. The last thing is that you have to run the thirty-three dive first and recently not in the distant past. If you do all these things right, then you will have a first down, a touchdown, or a very long play. If you miss any of these seemingly small details you will call me on the phone and say that play doesn't work. Then I will respond with, it does work, you didn't run it right or in the right place or at the right time. This is not your main play or your bread and butter play it is a very special play to be used for very special moments. Like fourth and goal, one point down and you need a two-point conversion. How about two minutes left in the game, fourth and one and you need a first down. Treat this play and a few more like the tight end scrape as if they were the golden goose, do that and they will continue to yield you golden eggs when you need a very big play.

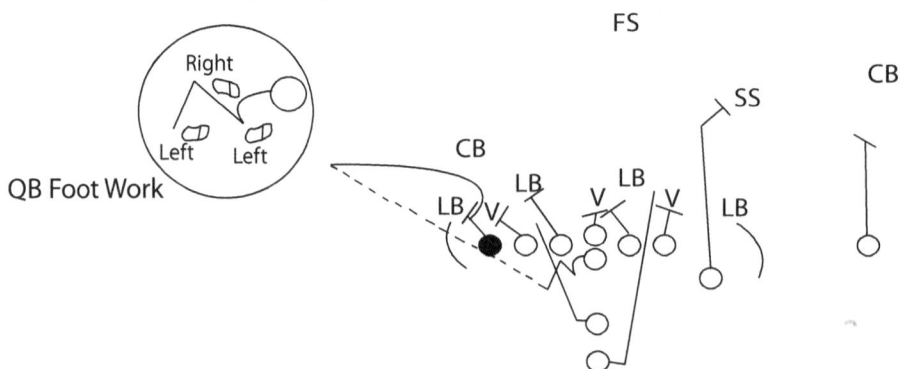

Offensive Summation

The pass thirty-three tight end delay will be the last offensive pass play I will show you for now, it is one of the most important plays I use but like all key plays the details are the most important.

As a side note, I have never used more than these few formations and plays to run every play I wanted and needed to win a game. You can add and change pass patterns to adjust to the defense but the basic plays stay the same. Keep in mind the old saying, *"KISS", Keep It Simple Stupid.* At one time I may have had as many as a hundred and forty-seven plays off these few formations and plays but I think it is better to run twenty-five plays great rather than forty well. I have seen a lot of plays on TV and watching other games and watch the quarterback go the wrong way. Then later see the wide receiver cut left when he was supposed to go right. If you make it too complicated or have too many plays you are inviting disaster. I can't say KISS enough times, you don't have to try to impress everybody with all these great plays and then lose the game, winning tells a much better story.

As you saw from the slot right twenty-four there are at least thirteen plays that start with that play and end up different. It is easy to add a little something to a play that works then to come up with a whole new play. I changed a forty-seven reverse to a pass play by adding a slot back post to the call. I can take the pass twenty-four and have the quarterback stop after the tailback goes by and throw a streak to the slot back. When you have a problem or you want to take advantage of a situation on the field, stop and think, be creative it will come to you when you need it. Maybe a different player can make a play work or a different pass pattern. Whatever, just sit back and let it flow and you will be surprised to find there is always a way to win a football game.

Chapter Two
Setting Up Your Defense

Defense is all about the basics. It's not going to matter what defense you run if and when you arrive at the point where the ball and the guy with the ball converge, if you can't make the tackle, all is for not. Teaching the basics will insure that when your guys are in the right position at the right time, they can complete the play. I can show you the way to line them up and the track they will take when the ball is snapped, but the basics will determine whether or not they can play defense.

To start off you want to set up your main defensive motto, mine is simply this:

One: prevent the score

Two: stop the run

Three: control the pass

You need to develop your own motto then base everything off of it.

When I first started coaching football I started with the defense we ran in high school which was the three four. However I found early on from an assistant coach that the split six had more to offer me. It had the tools I needed to get the job done more quickly. The three four is a very effective defense which we will look at a little later but to start we will look at the split six.

Split six

When parents, players and assistants first see me line up the kids in this defense they think I don't have a clue about football. Later in the year when we are still undefeated, parents come up to me and say, "great job, now how does that defense work?" Well let me show you.

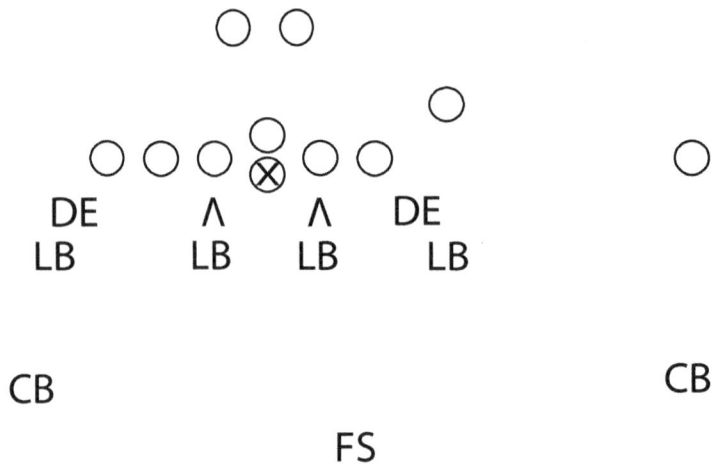

As you can see there are only two down linemen and four linebackers. There are two defensive ends that keep everything in the pocket and any backs coming out of the backfield. The outside linebacker stands behind the defensive end, then reads the play and reacts. The linebackers stand behind the linemen on the line and read as well unless they are on a blitz and that will depend on what I call.

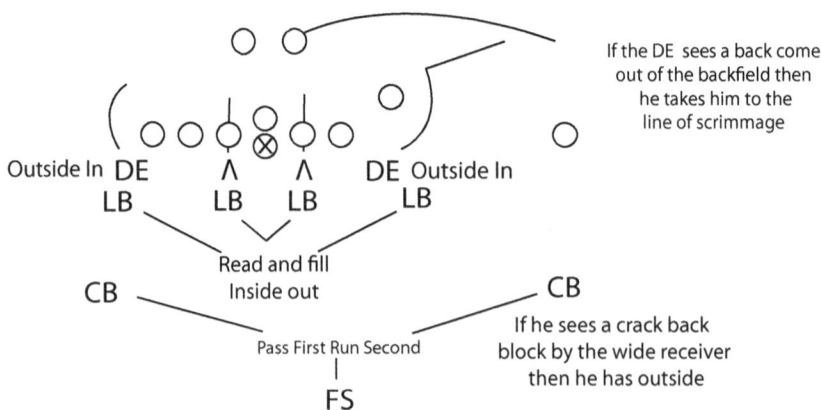

If the DE sees a back come out of the backfield then he takes him to the line of scrimmage

Outside In DE   ∧   ∧   DE Outside In
LB   LB LB   LB

Read and fill
Inside out

CB

Pass First Run Second

FS

CB

If he sees a crack back block by the wide receiver then he has outside

I can send all the linebackers or part from the same formation. If I want just the outside backers to blitz I call it a loop. I can send the right or the left outside linebackers independently or at the same time. Again whoever has outside containment either the defensive ends or when they are on a loop the outside linebackers will also have any backs that may come out of the backfield, whether it is in a pass pattern or whatever.

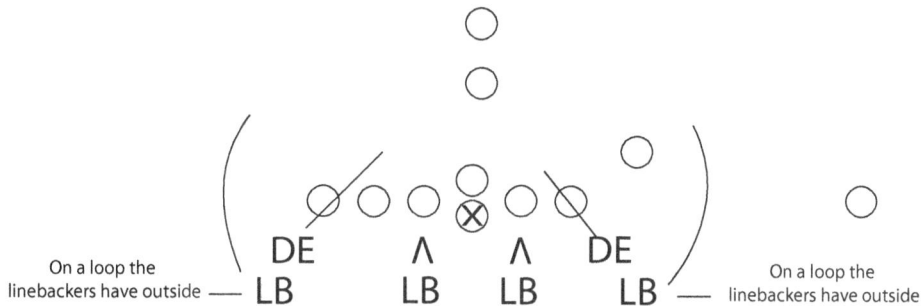

On a loop the linebackers have outside — DE ʌ ʌ DE — On a loop the linebackers have outside
LB LB LB LB

When the outside linebacker is on a blitz or loop the end crashes down on the tight end or tackle and the outside linebackers have the outside responsibility. The outside linebackers normally have an inside out attack, as the defensive ends have an outside in attack but on a loop they will switch. I will go over the inside out pursuit later as well as the outside in to show you why I use them but for now let's move on.

I don't use strong side or weak side calls for the defensive alignment. I find it's just as effective to leave the players on the same side every time; it gives them less to worry about and more time to understand their side of the formation. In the older ages you can go to a strong and weak side defensive line up because then you have a linebacker who can read and call the defense so the linemen and linebackers can line up in the proper formation. You can use hand and arm signals to call the plays from the sidelines.

Most of the time I leave the ends and outside linebackers to just play their regular read defense. I do send the two inside linebackers a lot more often. I can send them in many ways depending on the formation or down and distance or it will depend on what the other team is running, or if I just want to disrupt the play before it starts. I use hand and arm signals for this as well.

The linemen normally will just play a read defense unless they are on a blitz with the linebacker. When the linebackers are blitzing the linemen go the way of the call. So if I call a right side inside that means the right side linemen is going to the inside shoulder of the man he is over which is most of the time a guard. That means that the linebacker will take the outside shoulder of the same man. The same goes for the left side linemen and linebacker. The diagram shows all eight men are blitzing at the same time. That rarely happens because it is a little risky, but I have done it and I will probably do it again.

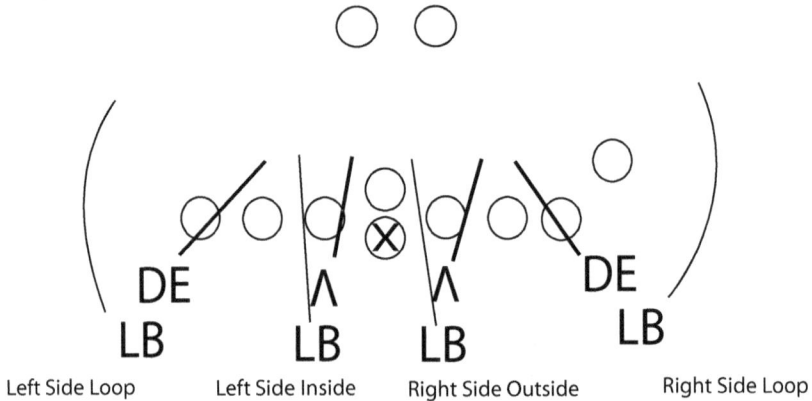

One thing I may want to caution you about is that you don't want to run a right side inside and a left side inside at the same time, it gets the two linemen converging on the center and it may get a little crowded in there but I have done it before when I thought it was a quarterback sneak, on the goal line.

Pass coverage

Split six zone

As far as pass coverage is concerned, I always run a zone defense. I don't agree with man-on-man coverage in the younger ages it has too much risk. The zone has always worked for me in the past but I don't want you to think it is the only way. I will show the man-on-man coverage just in case you want to run it in your program. In the older ages and definitely in professional football it can be run effectively but in youth football and maybe high school I would stay with zone and use man-on-man coverage on the goal line or in the red zone only.

The zone kicks in as soon as the defense can recognize pass. Unless the linebackers are on a blitz they will drop into coverage as well. The linebackers drop to about ten yards and have the underneath coverage. The three defensive backs drop and take the deep third of the field and as deep as the receivers. The two outside linebackers drop to the flats which is the area towards the sidelines.

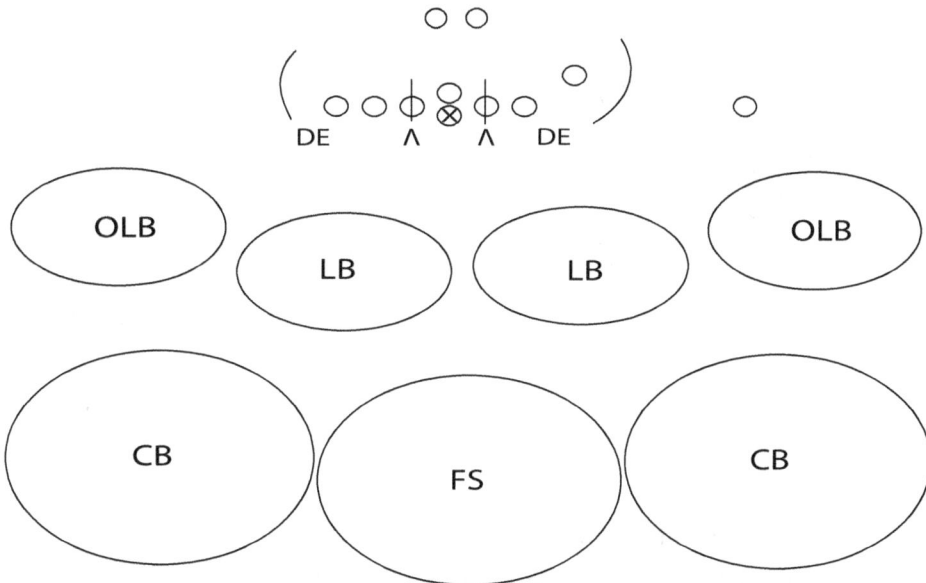

In a zone defense the backers keep one eye on the quarterback and one on the receiver, as the quarterback starts his arm forward the backs must fly to the ball or where they think the ball is going to go. Their job at that point is to try to intercept the pass, knock it down or separate the receiver from the ball. If the receiver catches the ball then last and surely not least, make the tackle.

I think of defense more as an offense. I don't wait for them to come to me I go after them. However I will take more of a soft approach outside the thirty-yard line. Then on special downs and when they cross the thirty I send in the troops to make things a little unhappy for the offense.

Spilt six man-on-man coverage
Assigning a man to each eligible receiver is all about whom you think will be best for the job. The good thing is that you can fashion your coverage to their ability. In other words you can put your best man on their best man however if you don't know who that is you can adjust to it after they score on you.

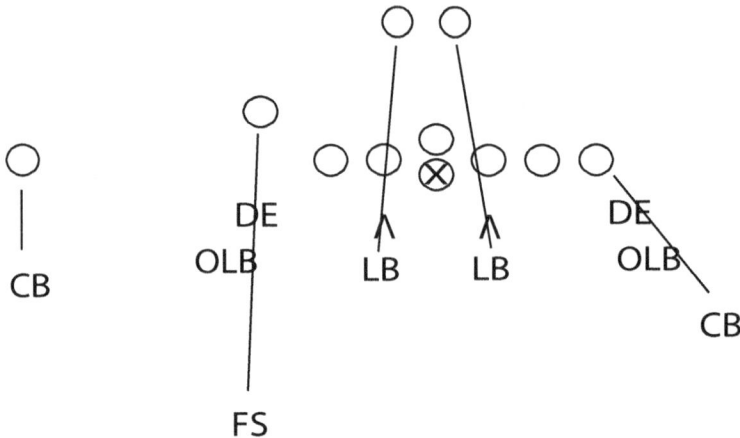

If you still want to run a man-on-man coverage let me give you a few things you will need to know. One, you will need to dedicate more practice time to teaching the basics about pass patterns. They need to recognize a pattern quickly and be able to anticipate the point of reception. That is where the quarterback will try to put the ball so the receiver can make the catch. The defensive back will have to be there before or at least at the same time as the receiver.

You want to be close to the receiver but not so close that the receiver can push off to create space. Even though this is not legal it is done on a regular basis and called very little of the time. I like to teach them to leave a little space and then close on the ball at the last second. If you are going for the ball you have a lot better chance to not be called for interference.

Now that you are at the point of reception their job will be to intercept the ball, knock it down or make the tackle as shown on the diagram. Man-on-man coverage will make it imperative that they make the tackle because there is no one to back them up. The rest of the team will be close to their man so by the time they see the pass, if they see the pass, they may not have time to help.

The rest of the team including the ones on the sidelines can help in this situation by yelling "ball" when the ball is in the air. This way the defensive backs can start looking for the ball and if it is not coming to their man they can leave that receiver and help with the other.

One other important point is if the defensive backs are trained to go for the interception at the point of reception then that will leave you open for the pump and go. You will have to teach the free safety to recognize that and fly to the go route. The go route is usually a high pass that will drop in for the receiver to run under. This leaves time for the free safety to get his butt over there and make the interception.

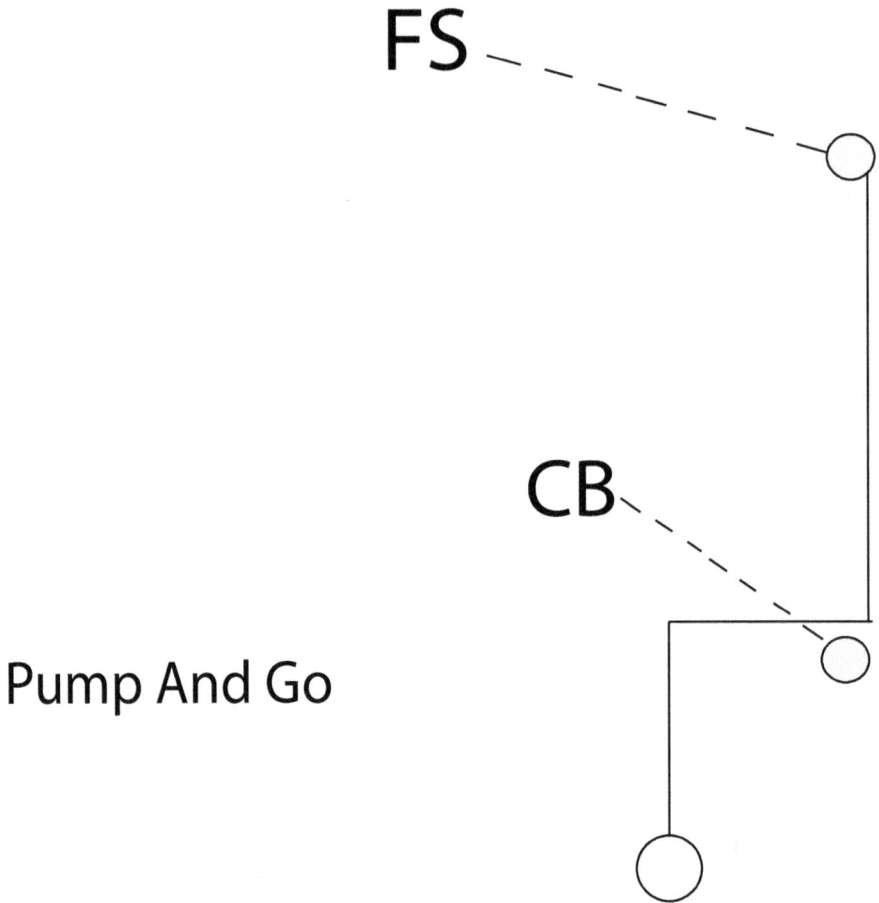

FS

CB

Pump And Go

A lot of these principles hold true with a zone as well, recognizing patterns, getting close to the man in your zone then closing on the ball when it is in the air. In zone coverage the defensive backs are always facing the ball or play so they can react to the play and close quickly. With a man-on-man as well as a zone it is very important to have the sideline players yelling ball if the ball is in the air or draw and screen or run. This way the rest of the team can leave their man and help with the play.

Three-four

Three-four regular

In the three-four there are three down linemen and four linebackers. You have a nose that will line up over the center. The right and left defensive guards are lined up over the offensive tackles. The two inside linebackers are over the two offensive guards and the two outside linebackers are over either the tight end or the outside shoulder of the tackle, depending on where the offense lines up. In the secondary there are three defensive backs and one strong safety. The defensive backs will line up on whatever receiver is on their side and the strong safety will be on the outside of the strong side of the formation. The free safety will stay back somewhere in the middle of the field. That is the basic line up. Different coaches will tell you different things on where they want them to go and which area each player has as a reasonability. The most common I have found is they will have a gap to protect. Some call it "A" gap or "B" gap. It is basically the space to one side or the other of the man they are closest to or over.

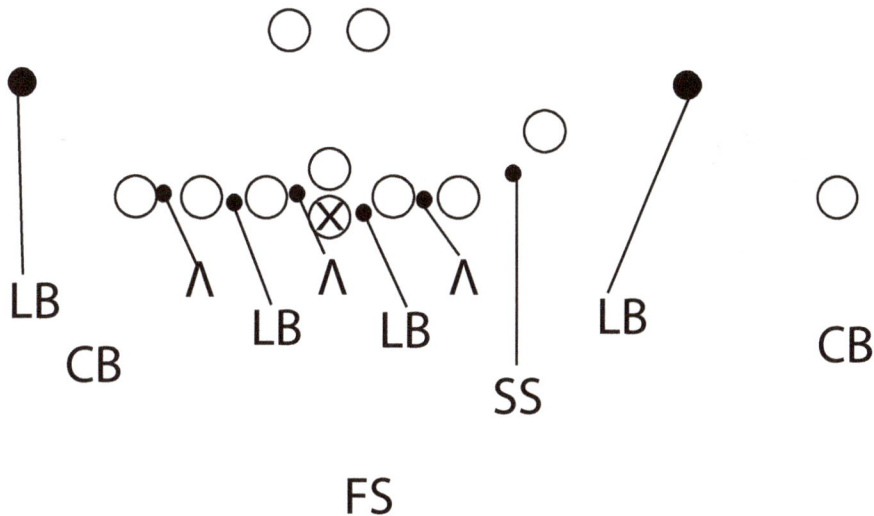

The strong safety can move around to different sides of the formation and can have different assignments in an effort to stop the run. He also can be set back in pass coverage to give you a four deep zone or man coverage.

This defense is primarily set up to stop the run. It is easy to see that this formation sets up a wall or a pocket to keep the play contained. This will leave only three defensive backs in pass coverage. It is just as easy to drop back into pass coverage from this defense as from the split six.

If you want to blitz there are many ways to do this from this line up, some will stunt or loop around the linemen or send the strong safety to different gaps. There are as many different approaches as there are good defensive coordinators. Look over these plays and then build yours from there.

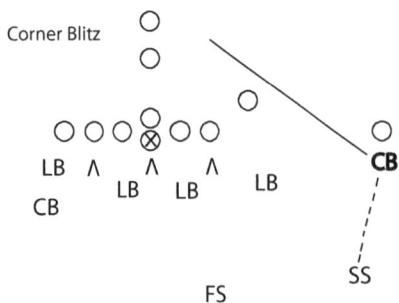

Corner Blitz

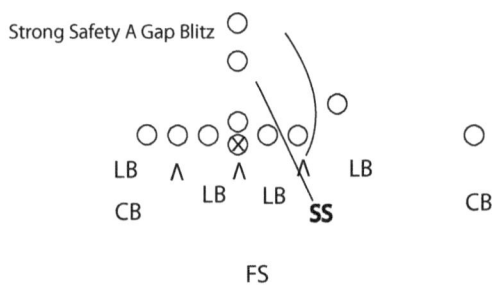

Strong Safety A Gap Blitz

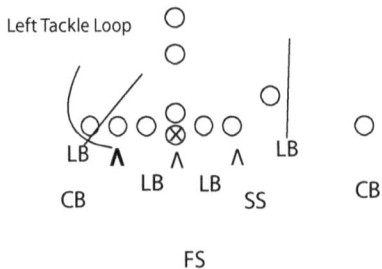

Left Tackle Loop

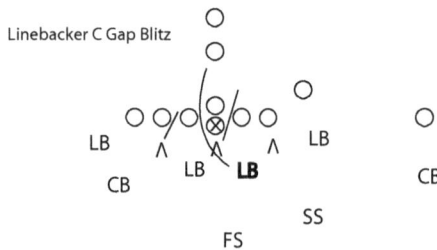

Linebacker C Gap Blitz

Three four pass coverage

Three and four deep zone

For a three deep zone the three defensive backs take the deep one-third of the field and the linebackers take the underneath coverage. The strong safety can take an underneath area as well or blitz.

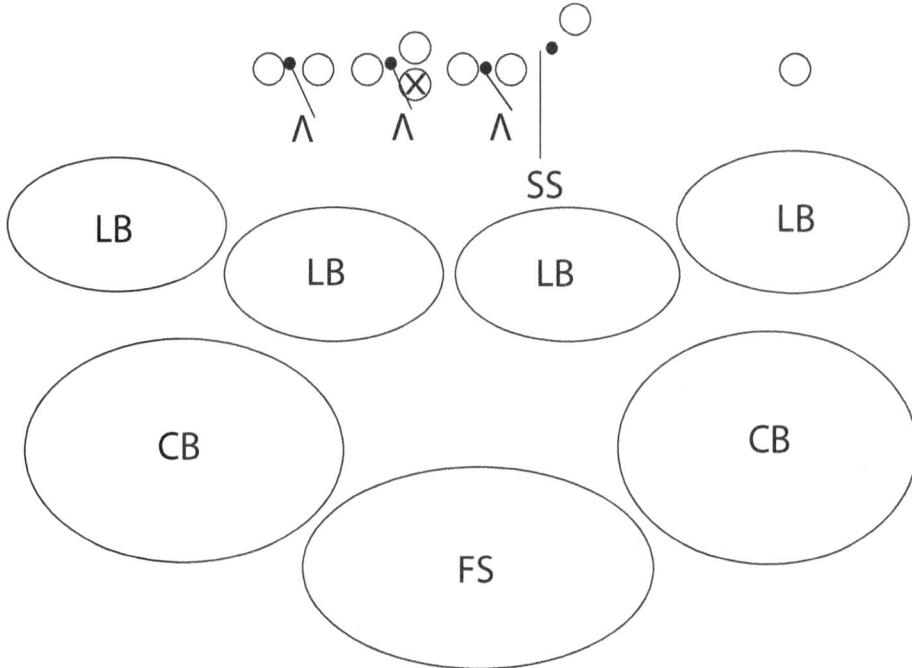

There are five eligible positions that can be set in a passing formation and conceivably be involved in a pass route, the wide receiver, slot back, tight end, fullback and tailback. If the team you are playing passes a lot then most defenses will take out the big strong safety and put in a faster defensive back which they still call a strong safety, and go with a four deep zone with the two safeties being the deepest and the two corners playing the deep outside.

That will leave you with just three down linemen on the rush. Then if they want to increase the rush they will send one of the corners or one of the safeties on a blitz.

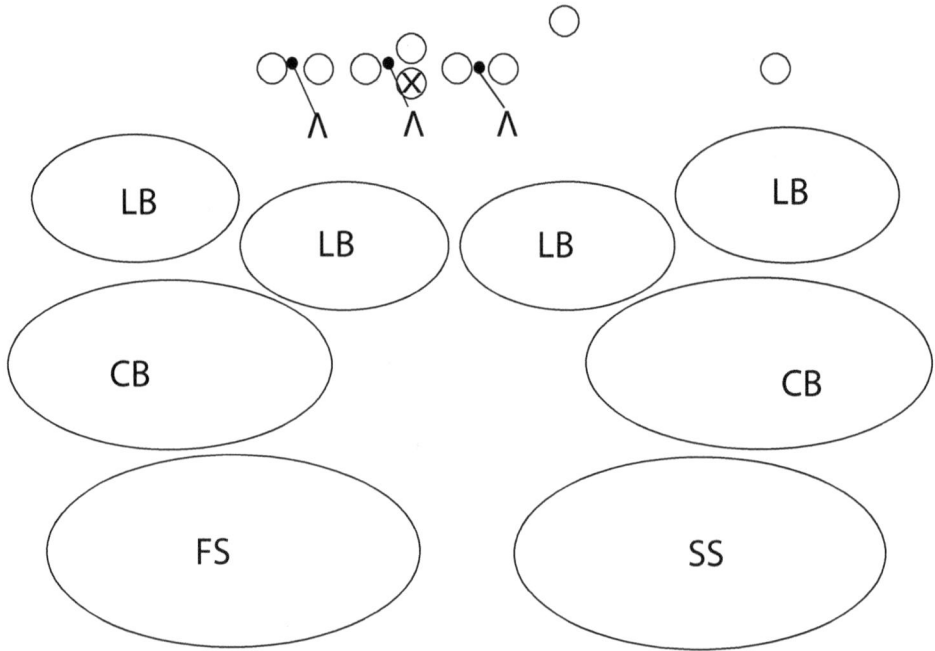

Man-on-man coverage

With a man-on-man coverage for the three-four is basically the same as the split six, each player is assigned to a man and he will go with him everywhere. The man you are assigned to cover is not as important as the ability to cover him. Knowing the pass routes they run, the formations they are most likely to run them from. This will help you in your pass coverage and overall defensive approach.

You can assign gaps to each position to help with identifying areas you want to attack, but this can change with every coach, some change the gap depending on the formation and first step of the quarterback. So this is just a jumping off point for you, take this information and try to adapt it to your system and remember the defense you run is not as important as the ability to get off the block and make the tackle. Teach the basics.

Chapter Three
Special Teams

The kicking game can be a very important part of your football program, some say it is one-third with the other two being offense and defense. The kicking game can turn a game around in crucial situations and change field position in one play. Putting your best players on special teams sends a message to the team that this is an important team, that we want the maximum effort. This is not somewhere to just put some guys in to unload the bench. This could be a very big play and something to work hard at.

Kick off

The kick off team has many applications depending on the situation during a game. The long deep kick, the squib kick, the onsides kick and the one I love, the keep it out of the star runners hands kick, which I call the open area kick. I can find no reasonable thinking process that would allow me to kick the ball to one of the other teams best runners. I think I would rather give up a few yards than take the risk of a long run back or touchdown and if I can get a shot at recovering the ball on a kick off then I think I will try that.

Long hard kick

Starting with the long hard kick, first of all if you can kick it out of the back of the opponent's end zone then do that. If not and even if you can each player on the kick off team will have a lane to cover with two or four players on contain. The contain players will make sure the runner cuts back to the inside and not go around the end and up the sidelines. The other six of the seven will come up the middle and fill in each lane to make the stop. The kicker is usually the safety who will play softer and wait for the runner to commit and then fill the hole.

Long Hard Kick

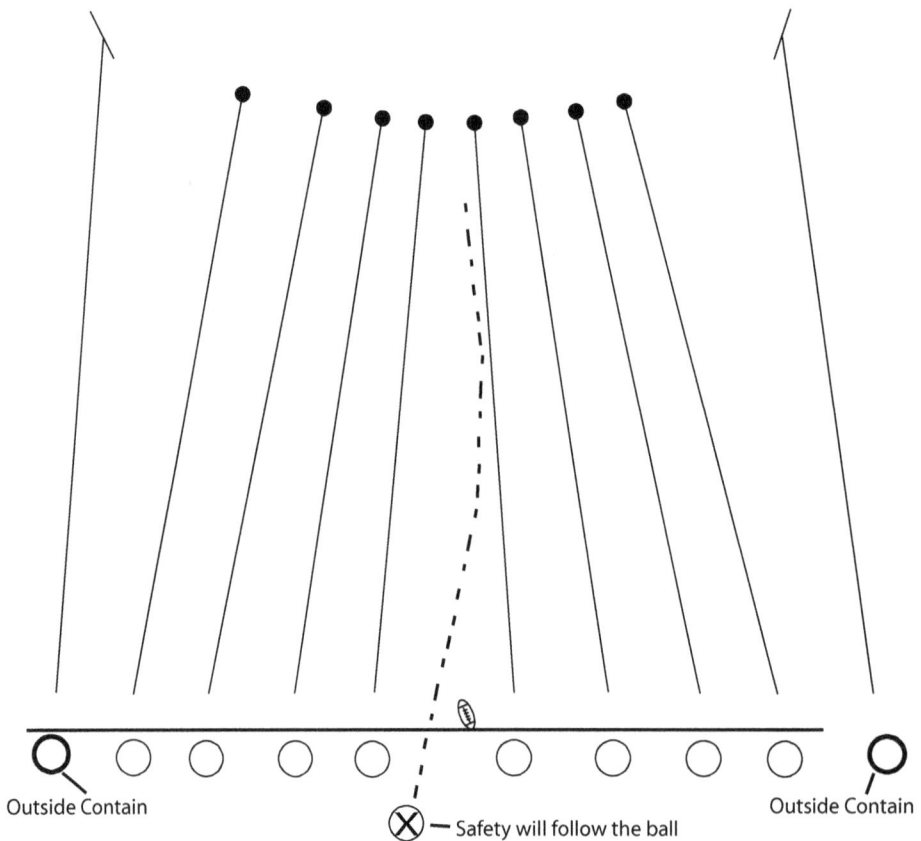

Outside Contain

Outside Contain

⊗ — Safety will follow the ball

Middle 8 must stay in their lanes
Two outside men need to turn the play into the middle 8

Onsides kick

The onsides kick is varied for every team, the point is to maintain possession of the ball. Most of the time you will overload one side with your fastest and best hands players. The kicker will angle the ball to that side from the opposite hash mark trying to get a good bounce that will give your team time to get under it and a chance to recover the ball.

The important thing is that the ball must go ten yards or more before it becomes live. The other is, if someone on the other side touches it then it will also be live.

I will still have two players to maintain the outside just in case someone from the other side picks it up and tries to run with it. I also leave two as safeties to do the same. One will be the kicker and the other will be someone that can make an open field tackle.

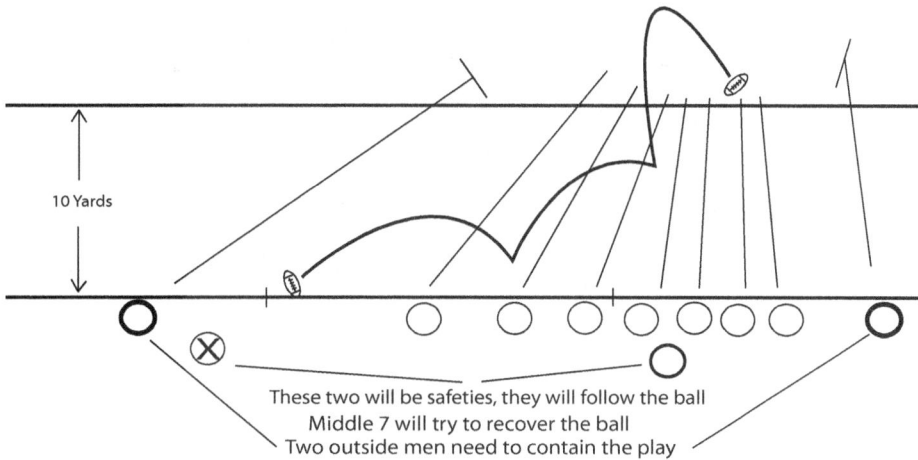

10 Yards

These two will be safeties, they will follow the ball
Middle 7 will try to recover the ball
Two outside men need to contain the play

Squib kick

The squib kick is a kick that travels along the ground and bounces around making it harder to pick up and disrupting the opposing teams designed return. This is achieved by placing the ball on the tee or the ground not in it's usual up right position. Rather on its side and set to an angle so that when the kicker's foot hits the ball it will start to spin and make it unpredictable as to where it might end up. This is still as hard as the kicker can kick the ball. The kick off team will still have its regular responsibilities as to lanes and outside contain, just the same as the long hard kick. There is no diagram for this kick, you line up the same as the long kick with lane assignments and outside contain, the only difference is the way you kick the ball and I did try to show that here.

Open area kick

On this kick you want to put the ball where there is no player and the most amount of open grass. I drew out the areas and gave each one a number so that when the kicker lines up to kick the ball I can signal to him where I want him to kick it, either by hand signal or before he takes the field. The rest of the team will line up the same as the long hard kick. I replaced the two or four outside players with players that have speed and good hands. They will try to recover the ball if possible, the rest will make sure that if the other team recovers the ball and tries to run with it they will be there to stop them.

The reason I like this kick the best is that it disrupts the return team and gives your team a chance at the ball. Another reason is when the receivers go for the ball it is on the ground and their heads are down and not looking at the oncoming defense that is about to kill them. About half the time we will recover the ball and the other half there will be little or no return.

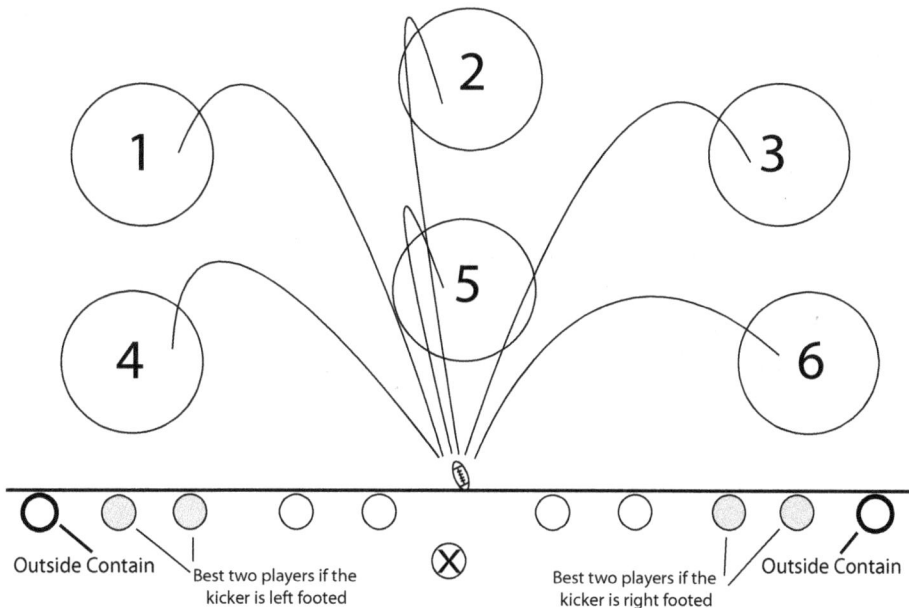

Outside Contain

Best two players if the kicker is left footed

Best two players if the kicker is right footed

Outside Contain

Kick off receive

On the kick off receive team there are a few plays you can run that will yield you some yards. The middle, the left and right side return, the reverse, the cross-field lateral and the miss direction. I have seen more but you don't want to make it too complicated if you don't have to.

The formation remains the same on most kick off receive lineups and you will start with five of your best blockers, fifteen yards back from the ball spaced out evenly across the front of the formation. Their job is to make sure the ball goes past them first, then form a wall either in the middle of the field or one side or the other depending on the return called. Twenty yards behind them spread out evenly across the field are three of your best blockers who can also catch the ball, and are fast enough to get to it. If the ball passes them they are to go back to the designated yard line and form a wall or a wedge to block for the runner. About twenty yards behind them are two of your best blockers that can also catch the ball but now must also be able to run with it as will. After the ball passes them they become the kick out men who will try to seal the defensive ends that have outside contain. The runner will key off them to make his cut. Just in front of the goal line is your fastest best runner you have that wants to be on the return team. His job is to catch the ball then run the play you called. If the ball goes over his head or he has to go into the end zone to catch the ball he is to down it in the end zone and get ready for the first play on offense.

Under no circumstances is he to bring the ball out of the end zone. Most certainly never when we are behind in a game and the clock is not our friend. When you down it in the end zone you get twenty yards free and no time off the clock, take it and set up your first play from scrimmage.

Kick Receive Formation

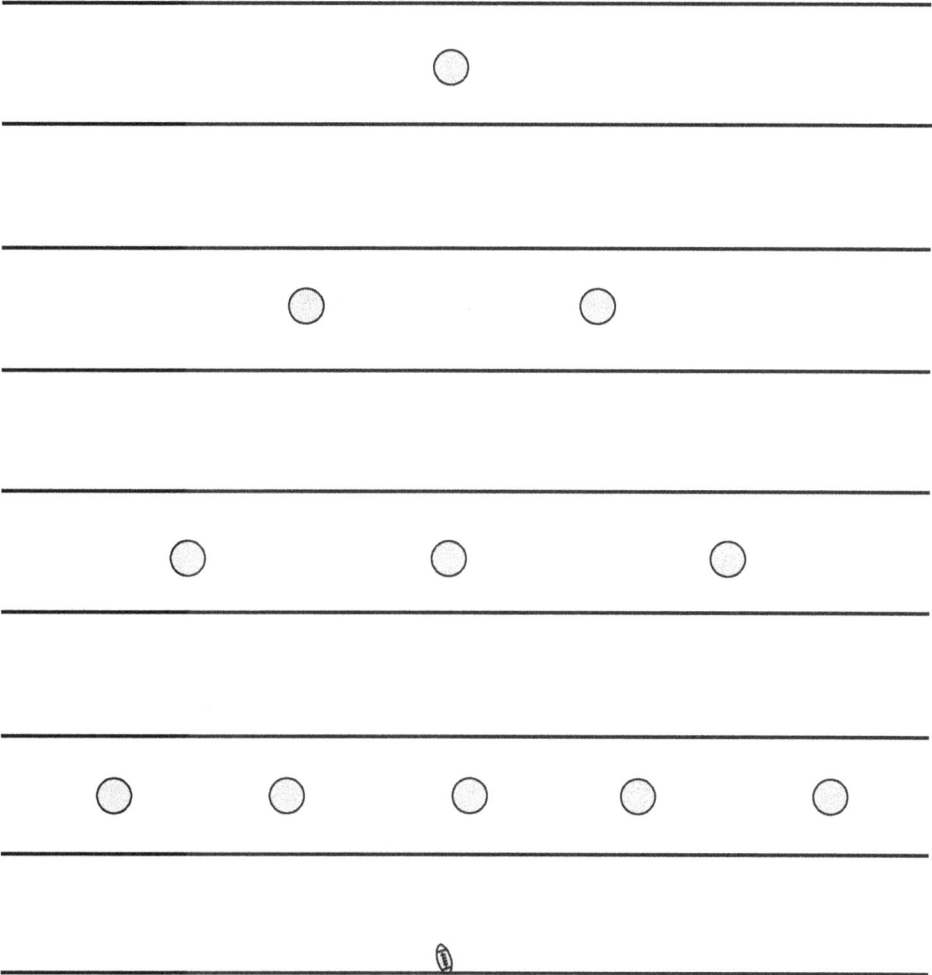

This is one of many possibilities, and formations you can use and run. I have seen many and most of them work. If you have one that you like you should use it. This is my favorite one that I use a lot but what will work for me may not work for you. Now let's go over a few returns to give you an idea of some of the many you can use.

Middle return

The five front will go back to the pre-determined yard line in the middle of the field and set up a wall from which to block from. The second wave will set up to kick out the outside contain defender in a crossing manner, while the two deeper blockers will go thru the whole and lead for the runner.

Middle Return

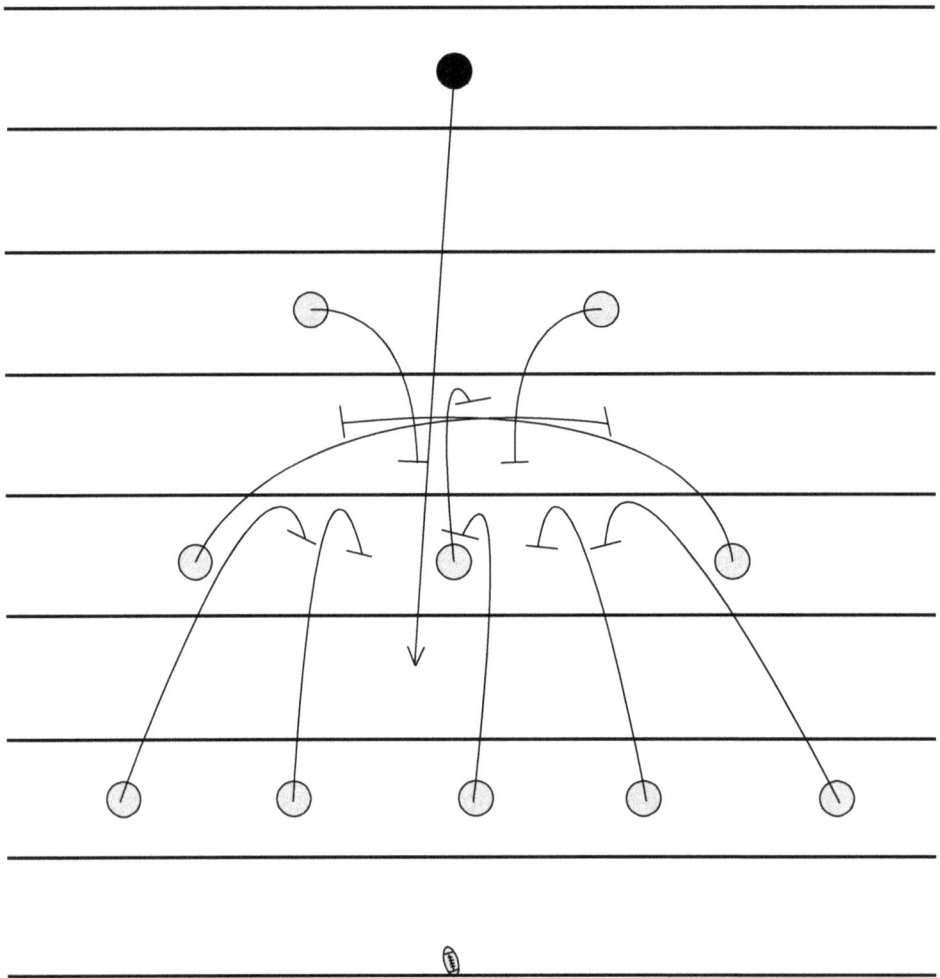

Left and right return

The formation remains the same but after the ball passes the first line of blockers they go to the side of the field that the play was called to and set up what is commonly called a picket fence. They line up along the side-lines about ten yards from the out of bounds line and block the man to their inside or downfield side. The next set of blockers does the same and continues the wall up field. The two remaining blockers will go behind the wall and lead block for the runner. The runner will try to get behind the two lead blockers behind the wall and run down the sideline.

Return Left

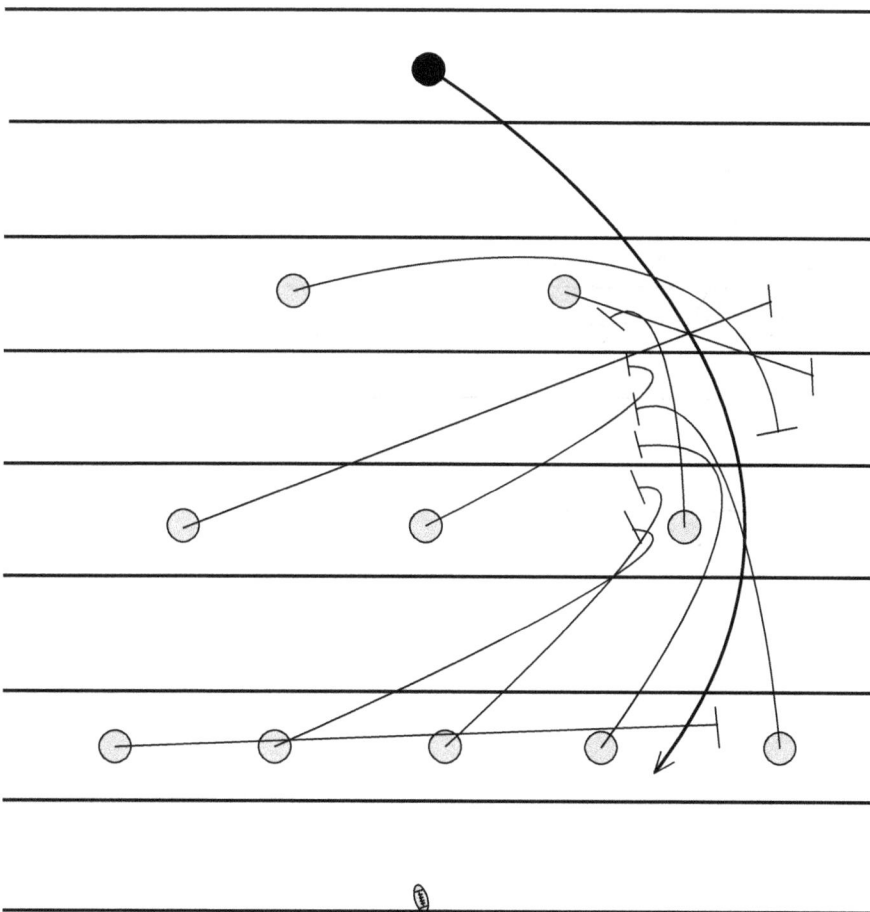

Return Right

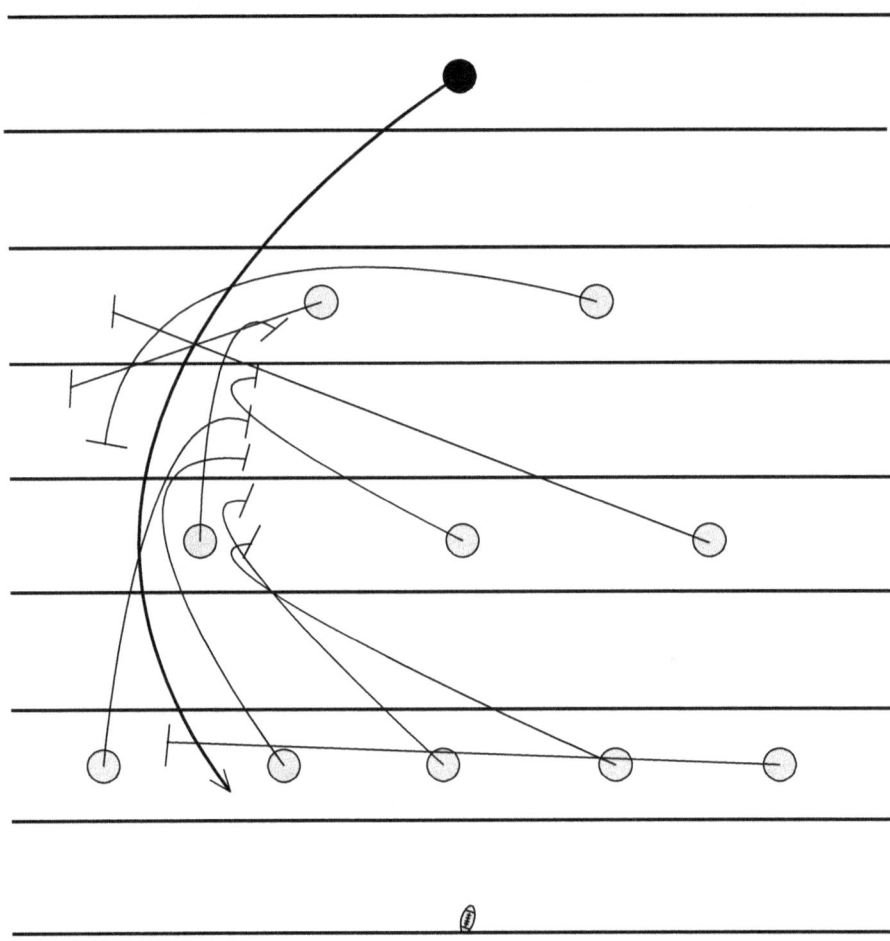

The Reverse

This is a two-phase play with different blocking assignments for both sides of the formation. Assign blockers into two groups, one for the fake and one for the reverse only use a few blockers for the reverse as to not tip off the defense. The runner will take the ball and run right or left depending on the call, then hands it off to the second runner who takes it in the other direction. The blockers you assigned to the reverse will wait for the second runner to come back their way before they throw their blocks. The runner will try to get behind the blockers who are waiting for him on the other side and run up the sideline and into the end zone.

Reverse Left

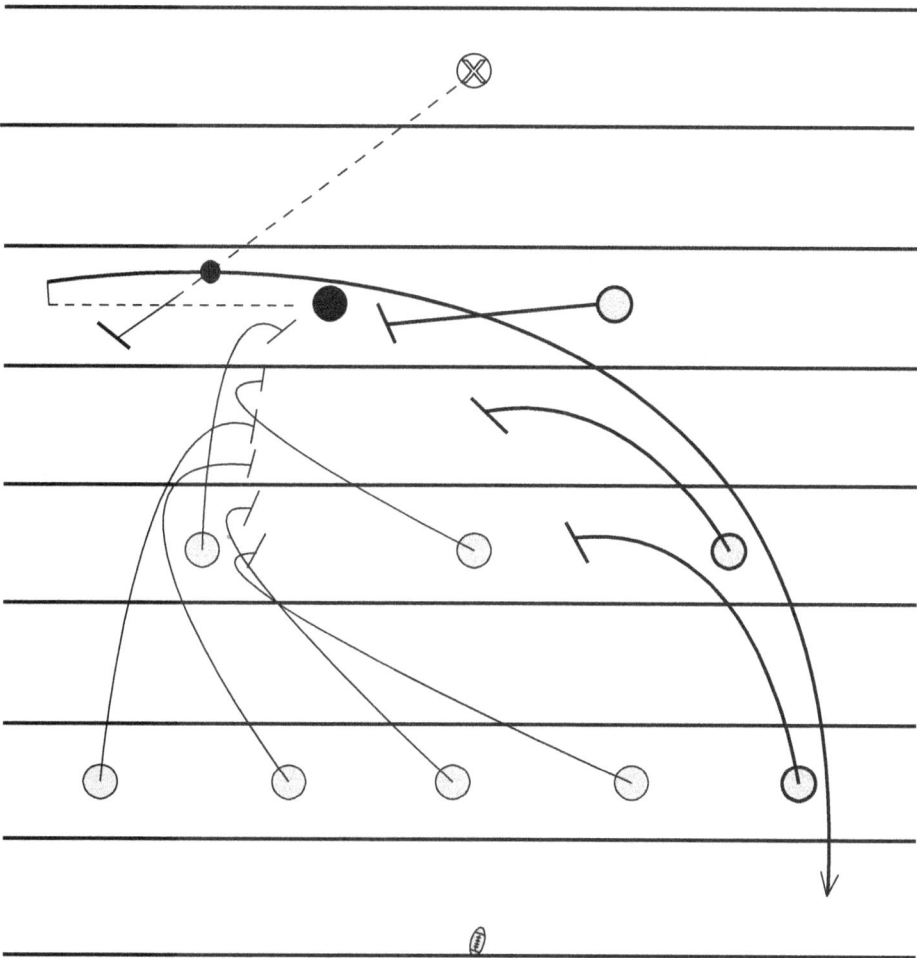

Cross-field lateral (Pass)

This play sets up a lot like a reverse but instead of the runner handing the ball off he throws it across the field to the runner who is waiting with a few blockers across the field. You don't want a lot of blockers on the side with the waiting receiver because that will just bring more defensive players with them. This is called a cross-field lateral because in order for it to be a legal play it cannot be a forward pass, the ball must be lateral or backwards from the line of scrimmage. However it is thrown like a pass because it has to go a long way. Side note: the ball is live on this play even if the receiver drops it.

Cross-field lateral (Pass)

Miss direction

I love this play the most but I try not to run it unless I really need a big play or points. The plays starts out like a left or right side return but you send a few blockers in the wrong direction or at least that is what you want it to look like to the defense. The runner takes as many steps to the one side or the wrong side as he can to draw the defense to him, then at the last second he cuts back behind the blocks that are waiting for him on the other side of the play. The two blockers that were in front of him lean to the runners cutback side and move forward downfield slowly waiting for the ball carrier to make his move, then as the blockers see the defense adjusting to the cutback they throw their blocks and the runner starts his way downfield picking up blocks from the rest of the wrong way Charleys. The longer and as much to the wrong side as the runner can get before he makes his cutback will give him more room to run behind his blocks. If the defense is not keeping their lane assignments (and how could they?) you will have a great shot at a touchdown. You want a fast runner on this play because after the cutback it is all about the speed.

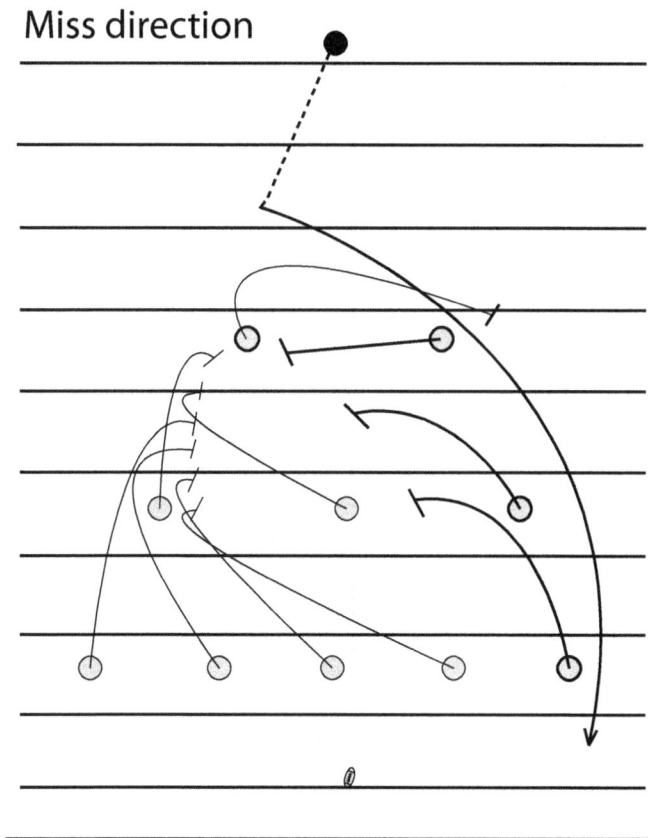

Miss direction

Punting the Ball

The regular punt formation is different for every team. Some will keep everybody in tight in a double wing formation. Others will send one, two, three or however many out wide to get downfield fast so they can cover the kick. Last but not least there is always the fake but for that I would rather just run one of my secret offensive plays. However you see it. The main thing is to not let the defense get to the kicker before he kicks the ball. The second is after the kick, get the guy with the ball.

Punt team

Some of the special teams are closely related to offense and defense. Punting to me is one of them. While I'm on offense and need to punt the ball, I will just use almost all of the players that are already on the field. I will send in the punter and take out the quarterback. Then go to a punt formation by putting the fullback and the slot back as wings and the tailback just behind the center as the play caller. The punter is about ten to twelve yards back depending on the age group and ability of the team. That is the only change I make.

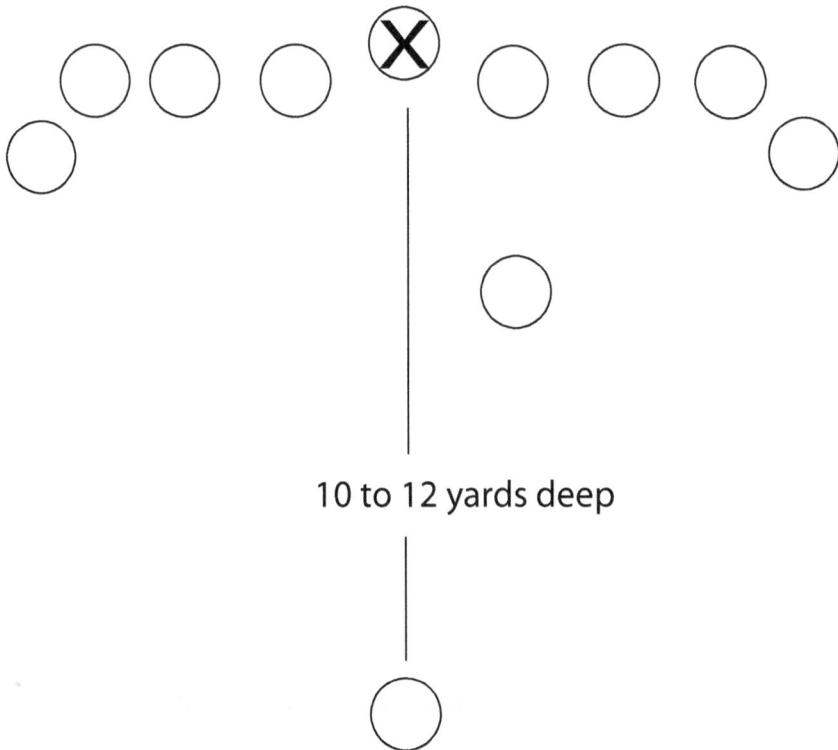

10 to 12 yards deep

One other formation I will show you at this point is the punt spread formation. This allows you to have two guys out wide so they can get downfield fast and cover the receiver as he catches the ball.

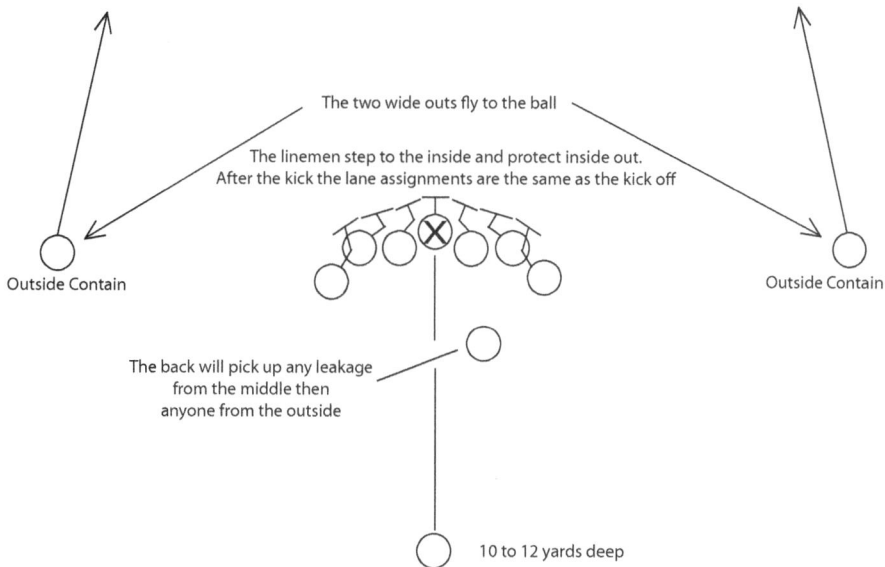

The two wide outs fly to the ball

The linemen step to the inside and protect inside out.
After the kick the lane assignments are the same as the kick off

Outside Contain

Outside Contain

The back will pick up any leakage
from the middle then
anyone from the outside

10 to 12 yards deep

The assignments for the linemen are to step to the inside and seal up the middle by forming a wall. After the ball is away the linemen will go downfield much the same way as the kick off team, staying in their lanes and making the tackle on the ball carrier. The two wide-outs are to get up field as fast as they can to cover the punt while maintaining the outside contain. The lone back will call the play and the snap count, then pick up any leakage from the center first, then look to the outside. When the ball is away then he will go up field and protect the middle. The punter will angle the ball away from the receiver and out of bounds as deep as he can. After he kicks the ball, he becomes the safety.

This works well in the younger ages because a lot of them play both ways. But if you are in the higher age groups you will want to use a special team for this. A team that is really fast and can make an open field tackle.

The only thing I am really sure about punting the ball is that I don't want to. If we have to, then kick it away from the runner or out of bounds. Kicking it out of bounds on a punt is not a penalty and it insures you will not have a return. The downside is you will probably not get as many yards because you are kicking at an angle and trying to hit the out-of-bounds line, that will also limit your chances for a nice roll. With that said weigh the risk against the reward and make you own decision.

On the chance you have a punter with a sixty-yard average and a fifteen-second hang time. Forget everything I just said and punt the ball straight and deep.

Quick kick

The quick kick is a punt play that I run from a slot right or spread right formation; however you can run it from any number of different formations. The basic principles are the same. You want to catch the defense off guard and get a long roll on the ball with no return.

The way I run the quick kick is the same formation as the slot right. The quarterback will line up the same but does not lean under the center to receive the ball, he will spread his legs a little more than usual and let the ball pass through his legs and go back to the tailback (which I replaced with the kicker). The tailback will cheat back a few yards then when he receives the snap he will take one step to the right then kick the ball. The fullback goes left on the snap count to get out of the way and pick up a block on the defensive end. The slot back takes the defensive end on his side. The rest of the line does their regular blocks and then goes down-field in the same way and with the same lane coverage as the kick off. The wide receiver and the tight end have to get downfield fast and have outside contain in the event the other team tries to pick up the ball and run with it.

Outside Contain

Outside Contain

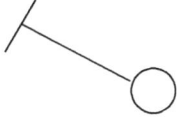

Safety ⬭ Tailback / punter cheats back a few yards
then steps to his right to kick the ball

Quick kick, spread

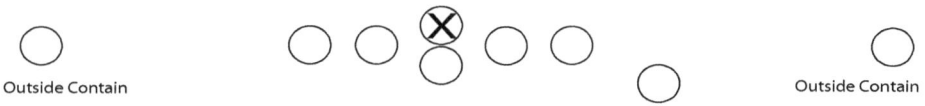

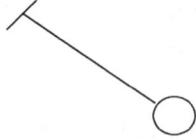

Outside Contain

Outside Contain

Safety ⬭ Tailback / Punter sneaks back a few yards
then steps to his right to kick the ball

Extra point

The formation on this play is very much like the first punt formation I showed you with the obvious differences being the holder and the kicker. The linemen will block to the inside as will as the backs, this will force everything to the outside.

Linemen block to the inside

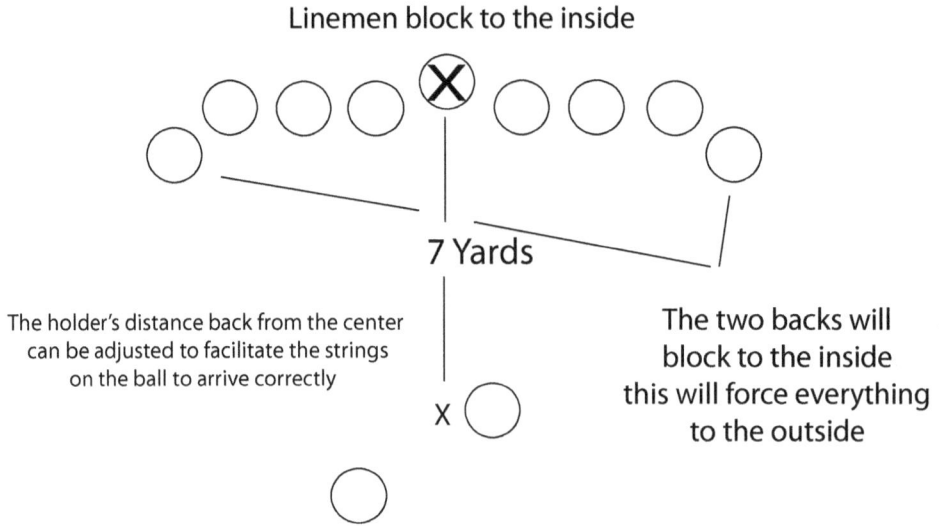

7 Yards

The holder's distance back from the center can be adjusted to facilitate the strings on the ball to arrive correctly

The two backs will block to the inside this will force everything to the outside

The holder's distance back from the center can be adjusted to facilitate the strings on the ball to arrive correctly. In other words the spin of the ball can be calculated to the same place every time so the holder can receive the ball strings up. However if you want this to happen on a consistent basis you must have the center and holder practice a lot.

Punt Receive

Punt receive formation

On the punt receive I leave the defensive team in and maybe send in a new safety to field the ball. I do this because if they fake the punt and try something new and exciting I want my defense on the field to stop it. I would rather get the ball with a few more yards to make up than to stay on defense. I have a number of great plays on offense which I love to run, but I can't if I don't have the ball.

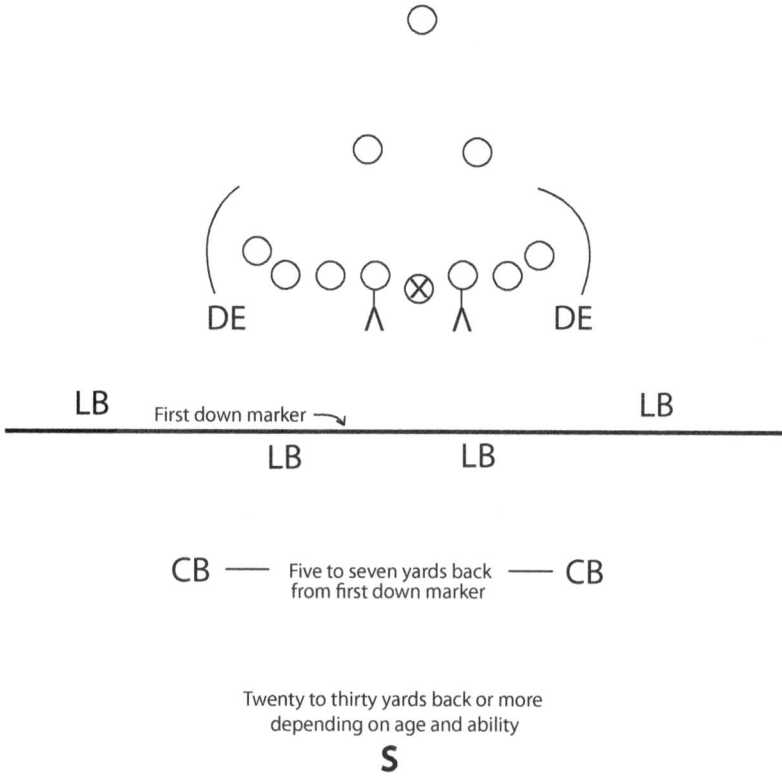

If the receiving team looks like a prevent defense that is because it is very much the same. I just have them drop back into a short pass coverage zone about five to ten yards back or close to the first down markers. After the ball is kicked I have the two corner backs drop back in front of the receiver and help with the protection. The linebackers will do the same just in front of the two corner backs. This is not a return just a protect play to help secure the ball for my offense.

Punt return

I don't have any big trick plays or fancy footwork to tell you about on this play, this is a high-risk play to start with and not worth taking any undo risks. I just tell the receiver to "catch the ball and if by chance you find yourself alone, run straight ahead and don't stop till someone stops you." I don't want the receiver to be thinking about the play or the blocks or anything. Just catch the ball. With that said let's set up a return.

To set up a punt return you need to find the man or men on defense that have outside responsibility. There are at least two of them. Put two or however many you need on them to slow them down and give your receiver time to get the ball and look up field. The rest of the team waits to make sure the ball is kicked and then they go back into coverage to help with the blocks. You would use the same principles as the kick off return. Left, right and middle. The miss direction, reverse and the lateral plays take a lot longer to develop and with a punt you will rarely have the time. Just simplify it and go with a regular return as shown in the kick-off section. This is the basic return to get you started and will help you get started if you want to develop a return of your own. You can use hand signals to send in the play (left, right?) if you want to wait to see how the punt team lines up first. (Don't look at this play as a whole, look at one player at a time.)

Punt Return Right

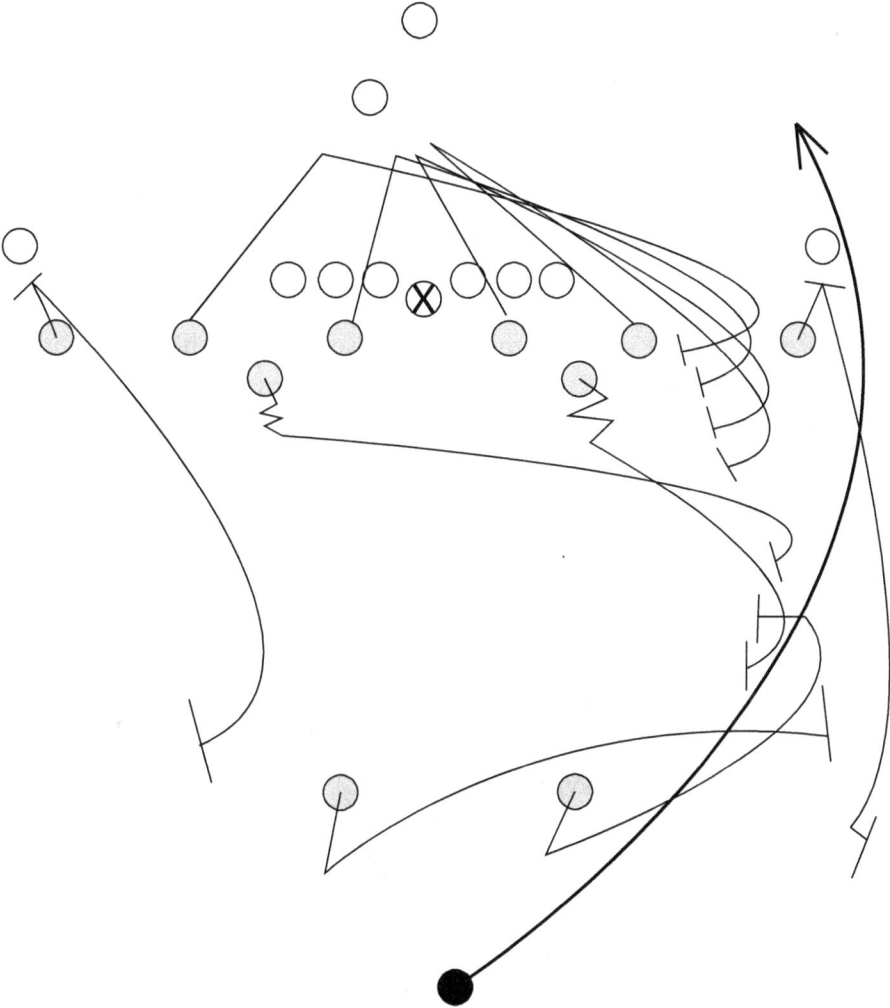

Punt block

Some teams put seven, eight and even nine players on the line in an effort to block the punt. I will show a couple of these but I find it too risky and prefer to just play defense and get the ball for my offense. I am also not in favor of a fifteen-yard penalty and an automatic first down for the punt team.

If you are putting on a block, the main thing to remember is to aim for where the ball will be kicked and not where the kicker is receiving the ball. Most of the time it will be about two to three yards in front of the kicker. If you can scout the other team you will be able to find that out in advance and practice it during the week. Also on a punt block you have nobody back to help the receiver so I would just have him do a fair catch rather than try to get a few yards and take the risk of a fumble or a big hit to give the defense a lift.

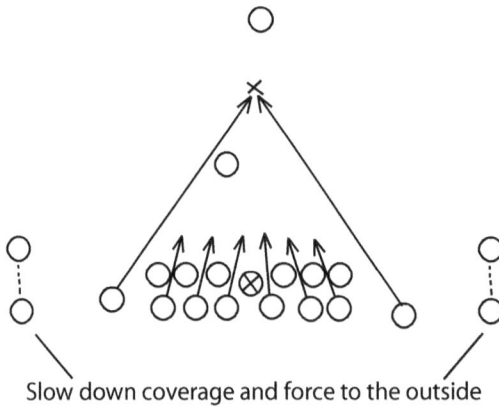

Slow down coverage and force to the outside

Twenty to thirty yards deep ● No return, fair catch only

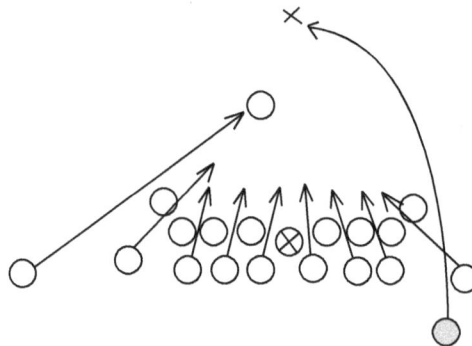

● No return, fair catch only

Chapter Four
First Step
Practice Schedule

Before you start to set up your practice schedule you need to know what rules your league has concerning the times, days, length of each practice and the most important, the first game. Some leagues only let you practice as little as three days a week after school starts, high school and up will practice everyday but Sunday. Once you have that information, start to go over the calendar for any holidays and things that might interfere with little Johnny coming to practice.

I have been on many practice fields going back 38 years. From eight year olds to college I have seen the good, the bad and the ugly. The good ones don't waste a single minute. Every drill, exercise and play is carefully thought out and executed. The bad ones spend most of the time trying to figure out what they should do next. Then the day before a game find out they are not ready, oh and we need some kind of defense and special teams. Then in a mad dash they try to put something together by placing kids on the line of scrimmage and tell them to get the guy with the ball. "Hey can anybody punt?" This concept holds true not just in football but in all kinds of situations when success is the only option. I was at a rehearsal for the Mormon Tabernacle Choir as they prepared for their Christmas program. Right in the middle of the practice the director stopped and said, "Ok the orchestra can take a ten minute break, be back here at eight eighteen." He didn't mean eight nineteen or eight twenty he meant eight eighteen. He had the entire night planned out to the second and any delay would set him back from his goal for the night. They had over five hundred performers and every leader of every group knew exactly what was expected of them to reach their goal by the night of the performance.

I was watching one of my sons' games in high school, when I saw them get called for a delay of game on the first play from scrimmage. Think about that. They didn't know what play to run, where to line up, the whole team was running around with the quarterback pointing and yelling trying to get a play off.

Long before the game is even close I know what play I want to run, the snap count, what players I want where. I make sure the whole team knows, that is including the parents, fans and probably the other team. I start every practice with the same plays on offense and defense. I just say, "line it up boys" and they know what to do. I can't remember ever starting a game with any play other than a slot right twenty-four. I don't care if the opposing team knows that. (However, just because the other team may know what play I'm going to run, it doesn't mean they can stop it.) Even if they do I have plays set up to take advantage of that knowledge they think they have. If you have read the rest of this book before getting to this point you already know that all I have to do is change one thing and it is a new play.

I start with twenty-four every time. If I want to change it because I see they may have adjusted to it, I just give the quarterback two words, "Keep it". Everybody on the team will run the twenty-four as always, but the quarterback tells the two back, "I'm keeping it", the two back will fake like he has the ball and the quarterback will keep it and around the end he goes. The defense charges the four hole and the quarterback slips out for a ten-yard gain. Oh I love this game, but more about that in later chapters. Everything is set up in advance, I try to leave nothing to chance. I want every minute accounted for and planned out as to what, where and when we will run drills, plays, offensive and defensive. I can always adjust the plan, but first I want to start from a place of certainty.

Setting up your month

I alternate days of the week with offense and defense. I usually put special teams on the last day of the week with some more offense. In little league I give a copy of the monthly practice and game schedule to each player to bring home to Mommy so she can plan dinner and get little Johnny to and from practice. In little league they will give you a game schedule, never retype it. I have seen mistakes on it and have had teams forfeit because of it. Always copy the one the league gives you that way you have someone else to blame.

August 2009

Sunday	Monday	Tuesday	Wednesday	Thursday	Friday	Saturday
						1 Offense Defense Special Teams 8:00 AM-9:30 AM
2	3 Offense 7:00 PM-8:30 PM	4 Defense 7:00 PM-8:30 PM	5 Offense 7:00 PM-8:30 PM	6 Defense 7:00 PM-8:30 PM	7 Offense Special Teams 7:00 PM-8:30 PM	8 Offense Defense Special Teams 8:00 AM-9:30 AM
9	10 Offense 7:00 PM-8:30 PM	11 Defense 7:00 PM-8:30 PM	12 Offense 7:00 PM-8:30 PM	13 Defense 7:00 PM-8:30 PM	14 Offense Special Teams 7:00 PM-8:30 PM	15 Offense Defense Special Teams 8:00 AM-9:30 AM
16	17 Offense 7:00 PM-8:30 PM	18 Defense 7:00 PM-8:30 PM	19 Offense 7:00 PM-8:30 PM	20 Defense 7:00 PM-8:30 PM	21 Offense Special Teams 7:00 PM-8:30 PM	22 Offense Defense Special Teams 8:00 AM-9:30 AM
23	24 Offense 7:00 PM-8:30 PM	25 Defense 7:00 PM-8:30 PM	26 Offense 7:00 PM-8:30 PM	27 Defense 7:00 PM-8:30 PM	28 Offense Special Teams 7:00 PM-8:30 PM	29 Offense Defense Special Teams 8:00 AM-9:30 AM
30	31 Offense 7:00 PM-8:30 PM					

September 2009

Sunday	Monday	Tuesday	Wednesday	Thursday	Friday	Saturday
		1 Uniforms Defense 7:00 PM-8:30 PM	2 Offense 7:00 PM-8:30 PM	3 Weigh Ins Defense 7:00 PM-8:30 PM	4 Offense Special Teams 7:00 PM-8:30 PM	5 Game Home
6	7 Offense 7:00 PM-8:30 PM	8 Defense 7:00 PM-8:30 PM	9 Offense 7:00 PM-8:30 PM	10 Defense 7:00 PM-8:30 PM	11 Offense Special Teams 7:00 PM-8:30 PM	12 Game
13	14 Offense 7:00 PM-8:30 PM	15 Defense 7:00 PM-8:30 PM	16 Offense 7:00 PM-8:30 PM	17 Defense 7:00 PM-8:30 PM	18 Offense Special Teams 7:00 PM-8:30 PM	19 Game
20	21 Offense 7:00 PM-8:30 PM	22 Defense 7:00 PM-8:30 PM	23 Offense 7:00 PM-8:30 PM	24 Defense 7:00 PM-8:30 PM	25 Offense Special Teams 7:00 PM-8:30 PM	26 Game Home
27	28 Offense 7:00 PM-8:30 PM	29 Defense 7:00 PM-8:30 PM	30 Offense 7:00 PM-8:30 PM			

After you have the monthly schedule completed you need to go to the daily schedule. This one can be made up day-by-day depending on how you are progressing. Here is a sample one to give you an idea but everyone is different depending on your program. If you look at the sample day schedule you will notice that I have every second accounted for. The only thing I don't have on there are the water breaks. You can add them if you like but I like to have them bring their own water bottles and drink when they need to. A lot of the time it is when I am setting up a drill or just talking or moving some cones. Depending on where you live that may determine your water breaks. Hotter, dryer climates may need more than Seattle. As you work your way through the sample schedule you will also see I start the practice as a team and then start to pull them apart to their different groups and then to their individual positions. On offensive days I use drills that are associated to offense and defensive days they are associated with defense. The beginning of practice is mostly the same for both days. We always start with team then break it down as the day goes and then at the end back to team.

Setting up day-to-day

First thing to do is to look over your playbook keeping in mind that offense takes twice as long as defense. Decide what your biggest play is, the one you base your offense on and start with that one. I try to get an idea of how many plays I want to have by a certain day. Then I work for that, sometimes I can do more and sometimes it takes longer. Don't get too concerned if it is taking longer. Just stick to your plan and keep going. You can make adjustments to the plan as you see how the team is learning.

Offense days	Defense days
5:00 Team stretch	**5:00** Team stretch
5:15 Team exercise jumping jacks, push ups, cotton pickers, sprints	**5:15** Team exercise jumping jacks, push ups, cotton pickers, sprints
5:30 Group drills carioca, monkey rolls, directionals, tackling drills open field one on one, two on one	**5:30** Group drills carioca, monkey rolls, directionals, tackling drills open field one on one, two on one
5:45 Individual drills running backs & receivers (tight ends) hand offs, pass patterns, foot work, gauntlet linemen (tight ends) keep low, fire out, alignment blocking assignments	**5:45** Individual drills defensive backs, linebackers linemen one on one, two on one, three on one pass coverage
6:00 Plays 24, pass 24, 33, pass 33 TE delay	**6:00** Defensive plays full pass coverage, blitzes, assignments
6:30 Full team offence run all plays as a team	**6:30** Full team defense run all plays
6:50 Run 10 perfect plays or run ladders	**6:50** Run 10 perfect plays or run ladders

Special teams
kick off, kick receive,
punt, punt receive,
trick plays

You can add special teams to
whatever day you think will be best.
I will use Friday and/or Saturday

You will also see that at the end of practice I have what I call ten perfect plays. I want to take a little time to tell you why I don't usually run after practice. It is mostly psychological. I don't want the team thinking about running more than the practice. I want them to give all they have during practice and not hold back. I tell them upfront, if you give 100% on every drill and every play we don't have to run sprints after practice. If I see people slaking then we will run and run till you, well you know what I mean.

Ten perfect plays is what I use instead, it works like this. On offense we run a play what ever it may be not necessarily with a defense. If it is run perfectly then that's one, if the play was not perfect then we start over. If they get to seven and someone drops the ball or something like that, then we start over at one. We run it in a two-minute drill setting (not an actual two minute drill that is run separate), run to the huddle, run to the line, run the play, and run back to the huddle. It puts emphasis on execution and hustle, they still run sprints they just don't know it, and this way it's more fun. Why just run when you can learn something at the same time.

On defensive days I run the blitzes and sometimes the offense. That will depend on how we are doing and what needs work.

On the sample schedule you will see different drills for different days. In the workbook I have drawn up some schedules and left some blank for you to fill in or use as an example.

The schedule is set up by the minute, I will have someone watch the clock for me or I will do it if I am not running one of the drills. I want everyone to feel like everything is under control at all times. I want them to feel like I know exactly what I am doing at all times. I want them to feel like when they come to practice they will learn a lot of football and be ready for the first game. I want them thinking about football before they leave the house, they don't have to say, "I wonder what we will do today". They know and they are ready for it because they know if yesterday was defense then today will be offense. Having a plan is mandatory. Remember you can always adjust your plan but only if you have one.

Whenever a player tells me that he has to miss practice I say, "That's ok but we will be learning a few new plays so when you get back you will have to work hard to catch up." That will shift the pressure off me and on them. It makes me look like the good guy and they will not want to miss practice in fear of losing their position on the team because their back up is going to be there and learning while they are at their auntie's house.

If a player is late I will not have him run around the field by himself. I would rather have him involved with the team and dish out the punishment as we go along in practice. "Since you were late you get to go first. Since you were late then you get the ball." After little Johnny has taken a beating all day during practice, Johnny and nobody else wants to be late tomorrow. Don't kill anybody and be nice, you want them to come back to practice and not be so afraid that you never see them again. It's not so much punishment as it is educational. Say it with a smile and a sense of compassion.

Organizational chart

Depending on how many assistant coaches you have this will determine how you break down your practices. First you will have to know which coaches you want to be over what positions. Take a look at the organizational chart to get an idea about how this might look.

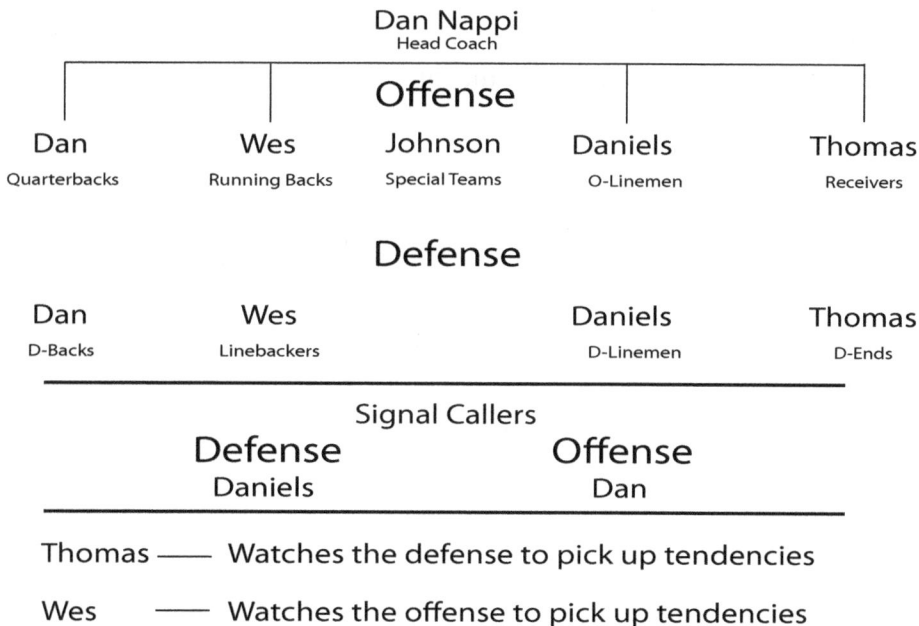

A chart like this will also help keep each coach focused on their responsibility and not worrying about who is going to take care of the linebackers. This will also help if they have a question about a position, they know who to talk to about it.

Practice schedule

Once you have the organizational chart you can set up the daily practice schedule and break it down even further to give the coaches exactly what you want. In high school and higher you will have more time to prepare and have meetings to decide this in advance. In the younger ages you will sometimes not have time to hold meetings to set things up before practice. With most of the coaches working at their regular jobs they cannot always get there on time. In these cases I will put together a sheet of paper to show where I want each coach to be at what time so if he has to work and gets there late he can jump right in and be productive immediately and not have to run around trying to catch up. I hand them a practice schedule and they can look at it and move directly to their area of responsibility with no delay.

Practice schedule complete

This schedule will break it down further and in more detail giving each coach a specific assignment in every area of the practice. After a while this would not be necessary because you have been working together a while and it will stay mainly the same throughout the year.

Offense

5:00 Team Stretch —————— Team captains (QB's and linebackers)
Jumping jacks, push ups, cotton pickers, leg lifts

5:15 Team Exercise —————— Head coach

5:30 Group drills
Carioca, monkey rolls, directionals, tackling drills

5:45 Individual drills

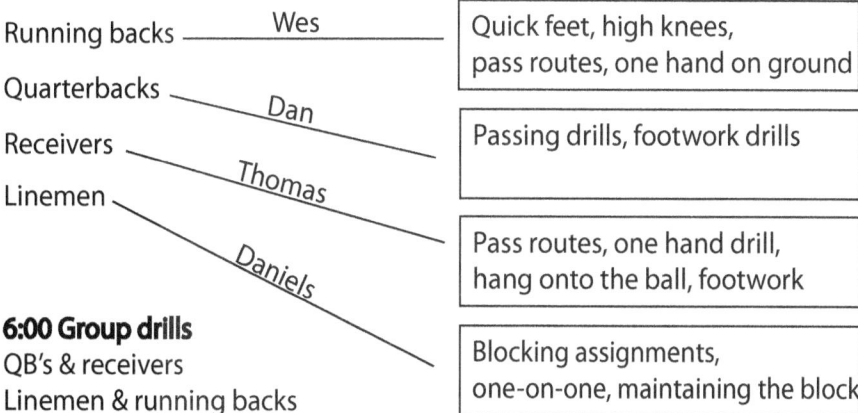

Running backs ——————— Wes —————— | Quick feet, high knees, pass routes, one hand on ground |

Quarterbacks ——————— Dan

Receivers ——————— Thomas | Passing drills, footwork drills |

Linemen ——————— Daniels | Pass routes, one hand drill, hang onto the ball, footwork |

6:00 Group drills
QB's & receivers

| Blocking assignments, one-on-one, maintaining the block |

Linemen & running backs
Split the QB's up with the running backs and receivers
and have them switch back after 15 minutes

6:30 Full Team offence
Run all plays, add five new plays

6:50 Run 10 perfect plays or run ladders

Special Teams
Kick off, kick receive, punt, punt receive, trick plays

You can add Special Teams to whatever day you think will be best. I will use Friday and/or Saturday.
If you are in the older ages and you have a coach for that, you can add that to the group drills.
However, I like to keep the teams together and run it as a team on defensive days.

Chapter Five
Drills

I broke down the drills section into two parts, before pads and after pads. There is only so much you can do before you put on the pads, but that doesn't mean you can't be productive without them. Also some drills are specific to a particular position, but you can decide if they will work for you in more than one spot, look for the side note on the title for position recommendation.

Before we get into drills let me first say a word or two about drills in general. Drills are and should be closely related to the type of program you are running, including the same snap count that you will be using during the year. For defense it should be the movement of the ball. This way they will start to become familiar with the sound of the snap count and to keep their eye on the ball for defense. Some of the drills may not be for you and you should use the ones that work for your program, and then design a few for yourself. Set up your drills to reflect your program that however does not apply to every drill, some drills are just drills that you want everybody to do like carioca, directionals, tip drills, monkey rolls, tackling, open field tackling and so on. You may want to see the DVD on drills because sometimes you just have to see it before you get it. The big example of that would be the monkey rolls, very hard to explain but real easy when you see it done.

Sometimes I will set up multiple drills and then rotate the team thru them every five to seven minutes, as long as I have enough coaches to supervise each drill, and get all of the players a chance at each drill.

Drills, Before Pads

One hand drill

This is just a short run anywhere from ten to twenty yards, putting one hand down on the ground every five or so yards. The key is to try to put some weight on the down hand, the more the better.

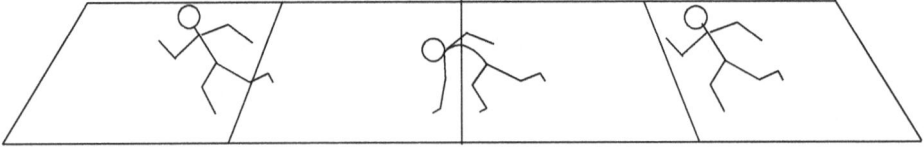

Running backwards

Just line up a few players and run backwards about ten to twenty yards then back to the start. Use the ball movement on this play and all drills that are related to defense.

One hand in a circle

The same as the one hand down but this time putting all your weight on the down hand and run around in a circle then back up and run to the finish.

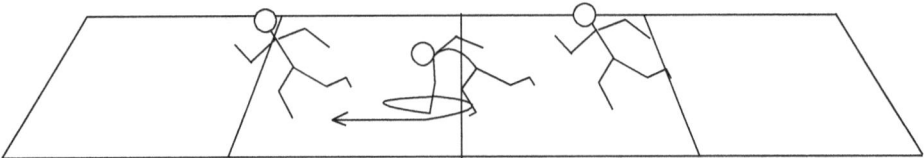

Carioca

Carioca is another one that is hard to explain but very easy when you see it done. It is a dance move but don't tell the players. Running sideways you put one foot in front of the other first then that same foot goes to the back like this.

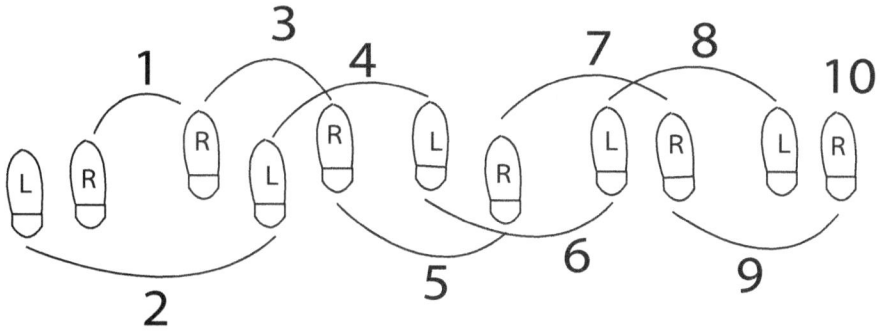

High knees

Run straight trying to bring your knees up as high as possible to your chest.

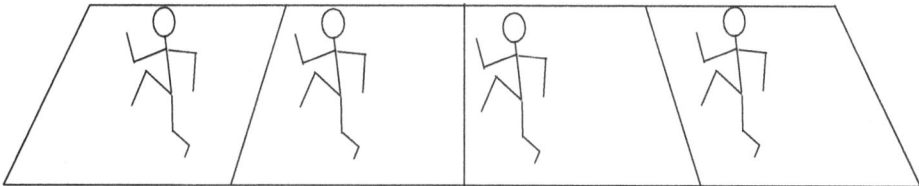

Monkey rolls

I tried to draw it up but after you see it you will definitely want to go to the DVD for this one. It is a must do drill with or without pads.

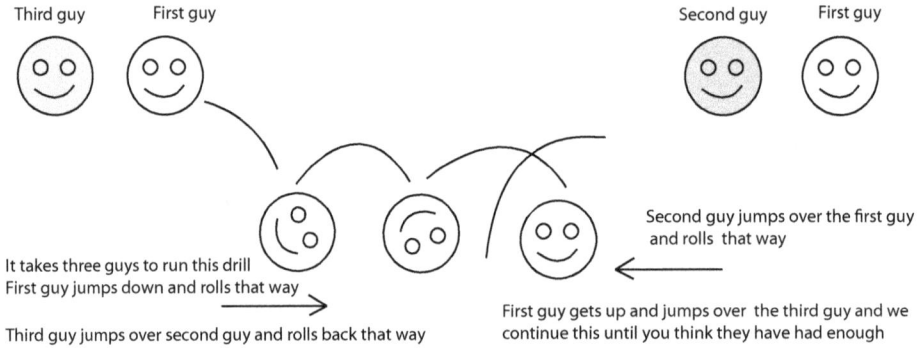

Third guy   First guy

Second guy   First guy

It takes three guys to run this drill
First guy jumps down and rolls that way

Third guy jumps over second guy and rolls back that way

Second guy jumps over the first guy and rolls that way

First guy gets up and jumps over the third guy and we continue this until you think they have had enough

Directionals

This is a very fun drill at least for me. I will stand with the ball in hand and as three or so players start to run in place. I move the ball from right to left, they start to run sideways in that direction, I move the ball from side-to-side as they change direction. After I am done I will throw the ball high in the air for them to run and catch it. Later in pads I will throw the ball on the ground for them to recover it.

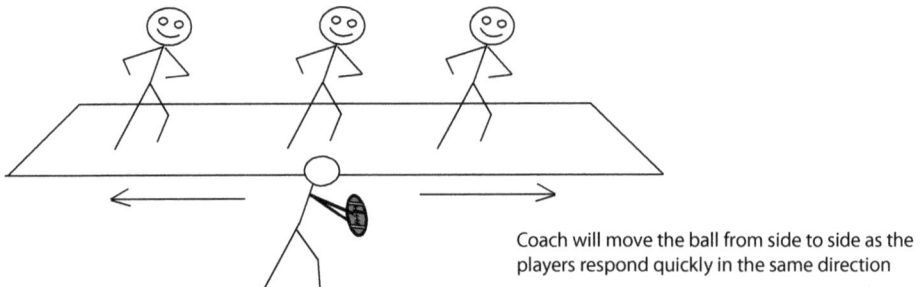

Coach will move the ball from side to side as the players respond quickly in the same direction

Directionals with a twist

Set up three tackling dummies about three yards apart, perpendicular to the line of scrimmage. Have three players facing you as you run the same drill as the directionals but this time they must step over the obstacles as they move from side-to-side.

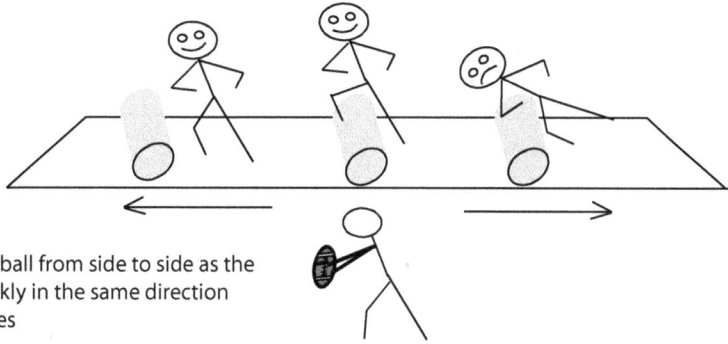

Coach will move the ball from side to side as the players respond quickly in the same direction avoiding the dummies

Quick feet

Set up some cones or markers about five yards apart and about five yards away and the last few close together. The runners will go thru the course as fast as they can without hitting the cones. When they get to the cones that are close together they will take smaller steps and faster.

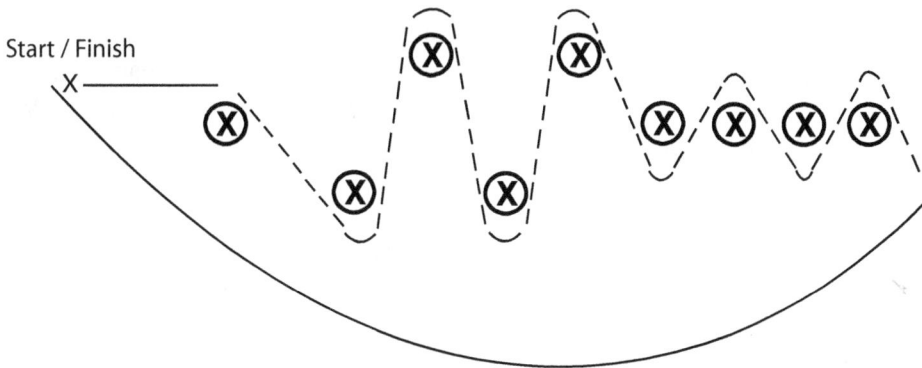

Start / Finish

Form tackling

Form two lines facing each other, one is the ball carrier and the other is the tackler. The objective is to get into position and understand the proper technique for making a tackle. Which is to keep your feet apart as you come across the body with your head, and to wrap your arms around the waist of the ball carrier driving him up and back. This also is run in slow motion until you get pads on. If you have a tackling dummy and you want to avoid injuries I would do that until you get in pads.

Tire pressure

Take some old bicycle tubes if you can find a few and put it around the waist of the first runner. The second man will hold the tube and keep pressure on it so the runner has to pull him along. After they reach the other side they will switch and run back. I have also see it done with old tires and they just drag the tire ten or more yards and back.

One knee passing (Quarterbacks)

Put the quarterbacks on one knee and have them pass the ball to a receiver or another quarterback. This will help analyze their throwing motion, give them some practice with their throwing and see how strong their arms are.

Pass routes (backs & receivers)

Set up on the sidelines or with cones and mark the pass pattern you want to run. Make sure they stay on the lines and markers so that the pattern is the same for everyone. You or the quarterback will throw the ball at the end of the pattern.

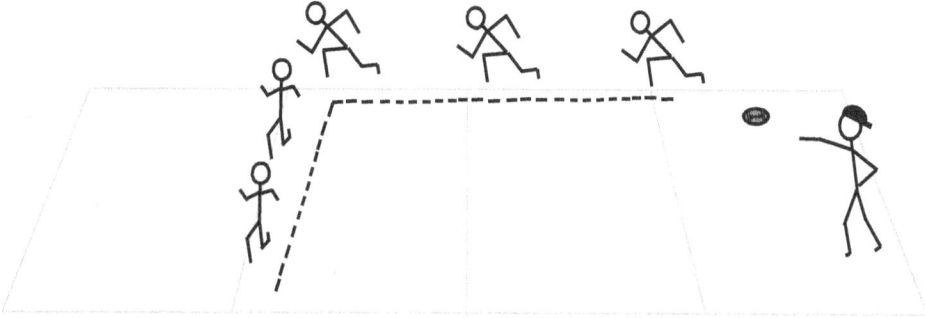

Pass routes (backs & receivers)

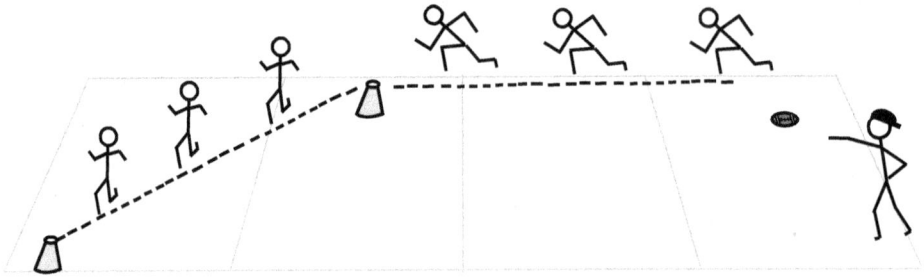

Pass patterns (backs & receivers)

You or one of the quarterbacks will throw the ball to players on a plethora of your own pass patterns. This could be run with all players, it is a good way to run and have fun at the same time.

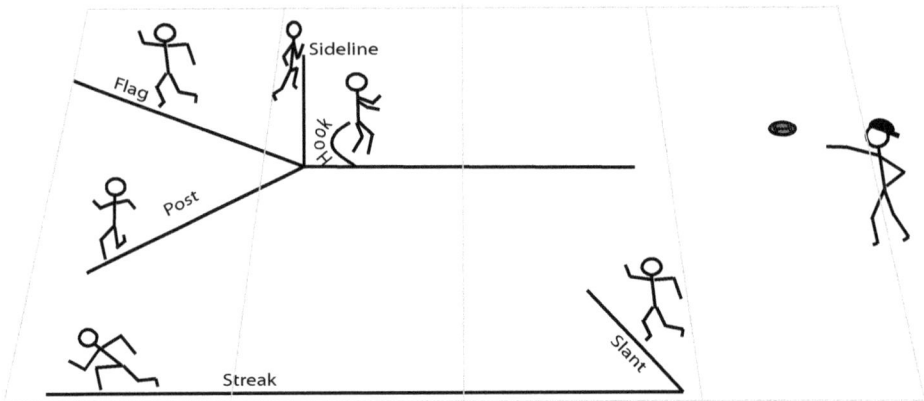

Back-to-back

I will have more than one line and if I want to use this drill as a warm-up or just to run the team I will use assistant coaches to throw the ball. (Ten push-ups if they drop the ball.)

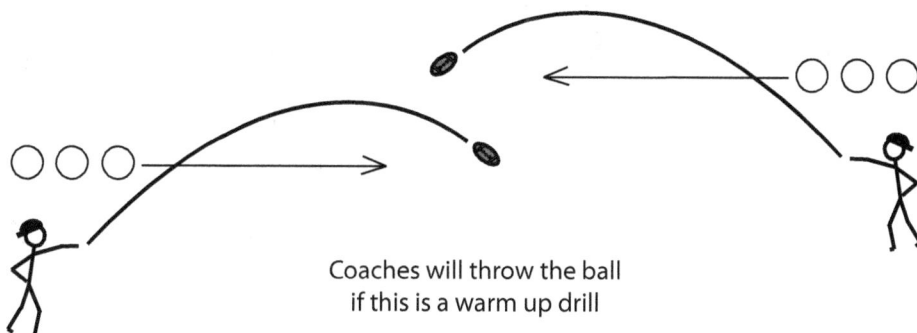

Coaches will throw the ball
if this is a warm up drill

Concentration (back & receivers)

Two lines facing one another, one line is the receiver and the other is the distracter. I will throw the ball to the receivers as the distracters run in the opposing direction towards the receiver and putting their hands up as close to the ball as they can without touching it. He is trying to break his concentration by getting as close to the ball and the receiver as possible without touching either one.

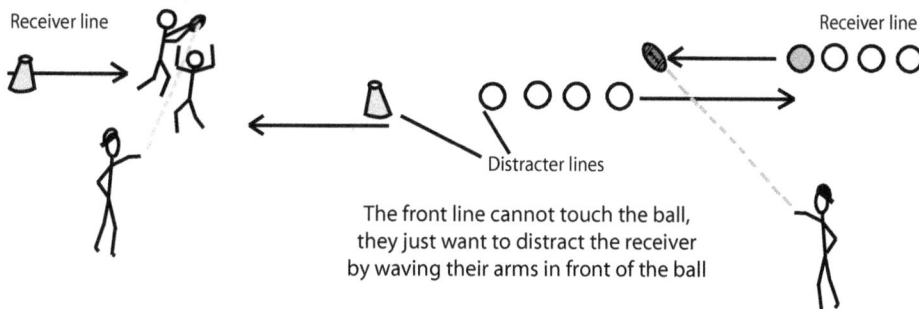

Receiver line   Receiver line

Distracter lines

The front line cannot touch the ball,
they just want to distract the receiver
by waving their arms in front of the ball

Ball control (backs & receivers)

This drill is a lot like the concentration drill but the second line is at the end of the catch and they will try to knock the ball out of the receiver's hands after he catches it. After pads they can hit the receiver after the catch, but cannot knock him down or tackle him.

They try to knock the ball loose, if they are in pads they can hit the receiver after he catches the ball but not tackle him or knock him down

Four square

This is the same principle as the back-to-back but covering a larger area. I form four lines about twenty to thirty yards apart or more (depending on age) for each side and run the team in a square. As they catch the ball they will hand it to the next receiver and get in the back of that line.

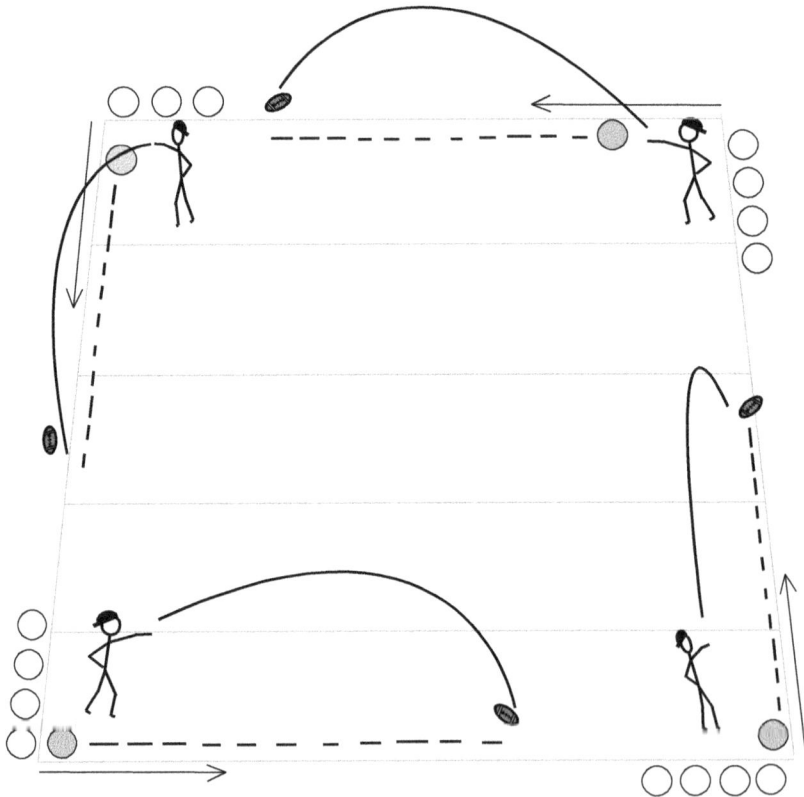

One hand catch (backs & receivers)

Two lines, one is a right hand catch and the other a left hand catch, going in the same direction perpendicular to the line of scrimmage. You can have two quarterbacks or you can alternate from left to right. One line is for the left hand and the other is for the right hand. Each receiver will catch the ball with the outside hand only then pull the ball into his chest and secure it with both hands.

Outside hand only

Tip drill (receivers & defensive backs)

I don't know anyone that doesn't do this one. Form one line facing you then the two players run towards you as you throw the ball at the first player. He tips the ball in the air and then the second guy who is running behind him will try to catch it. I have seen some coaches put more kids in front of the receiver and the ball will be tipped up around a few times before the last guy tries to catch it.

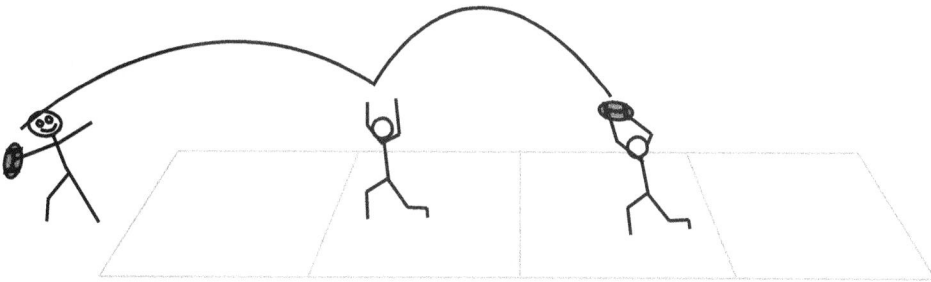

Three deep (defensive backs & linebackers)
Put three backs facing you and then at the snap of the ball they start running backwards, as you move the ball from left to right in a passing stance the backs will angle to that side still going backwards keeping their eyes on the ball and their shoulders facing forwards as they run back. After they have got back deep enough you will throw the ball just far enough in their reach to catch it but not right at them. Make them work to get the ball. If they drop the ball or don't get close enough to it, all three must do ten push up's (you are the judge if it was catchable or not).

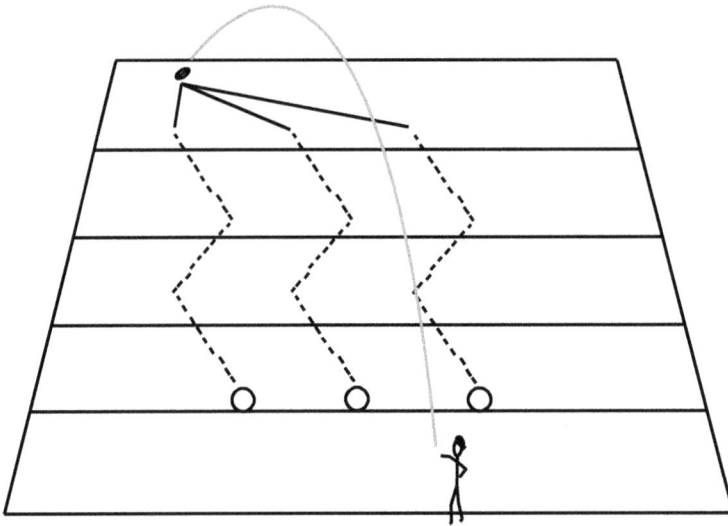

Side view

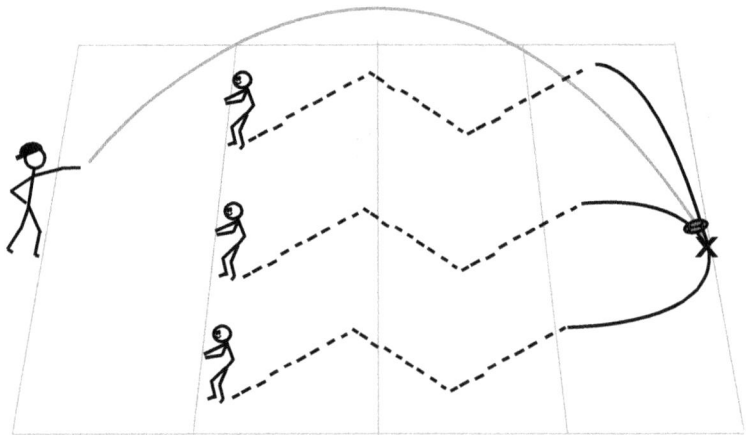

Drills, after pads

Form tackling with pads

Set up markers for two lines about five yards apart facing each other. One line is the ball carrier and the other is the tackler. Just like the non-pad drill you want to get your head across the body of the ball carrier and drive him back. The key points are to not leave your feet and drive the ball carrier back away from the line of scrimmage and from getting any yards.

Two-on-one

This is the most important drill I know of, if you can't get them to do this drill correctly you will have a very sad year. Everyone but the linemen will stand up on this drill other than that the concept remains the same for all. It is also different for the defensive end as well. First thing to remember is that there is a hole to protect or for the defensive ends an area of responsibility to maintain.

First set up markers about three yards apart this may vary depending on age and position. There is a ball carrier and a blocker in front of him. The tackler will be in the hole and he is to not let the ball carrier thru it. He must first take on the blocker and then drive the ball carrier back with no yards gained. The first thing that tacklers will want to do is to step to one side and try to go around the blocker. This is so wrong on many different levels. One, by stepping to one side you already gave up the hole to the blocker and his coach will say great job son but he really didn't do anything the tackler gave him the hole. **He must not leave the hole.**

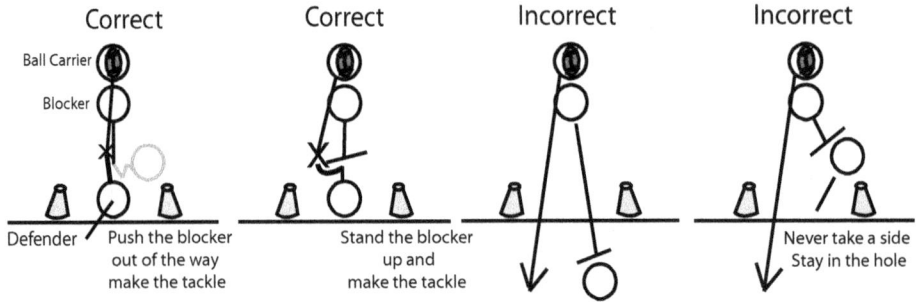

Correct | Correct | Incorrect | Incorrect

Ball Carrier
Blocker
Defender
Push the blocker out of the way make the tackle
Stand the blocker up and make the tackle
Never take a side Stay in the hole

To start, the runner will be about five yards back from the hole, the blocker is just in front of him. They start towards the hole the defender will stand the blocker up and push him to one side or the other. Then he hits the runner across the numbers and drives him back into the backfield. That is the perfect execution of the drill, but as you may know it will take some-time to get there. One thing I will accept is that if the defender can stand up the blocker and give no room for the runner to get thru the hole for two or three seconds that will do for his turn. The runner must go thru the hole and not around the markers. Most of the team should be able to do this with no trouble; there will always be a few that will play only offense.

Three-on-one plus

Now the fun begins with this three-on-one and four-on-one and so on until you just have a few left that will stand in there and take the hits for the glory and the fame. This drill is not for everyone but there are a few that want and love to hit and they are your first string defense. After you get past four you will want to let the ones sit out that don't feel this is for them. It is better than losing half your team and have them back down from hitting at their level. I don't make it sound like they are wimps I just say, "Who wants to go for five? Who's left for the six o'clock call? All right let's do this!" This is not a hit and let go drill the defender must stand in the hole and not let anyone thru. The blockers only get one hit, then they step to one side to make way for the second, third and so on, there is only a few that can get this done so don't expect too much. However for a real good time watch the DVD.

Correct   Correct   Incorrect   Incorrect

Ball Carrier

Blocker

Blocker

Defender   Push the blocker   Stand the blocker   Never take a side
            out of the way   up and   Stay in the hole
            make the tackle   make the tackle

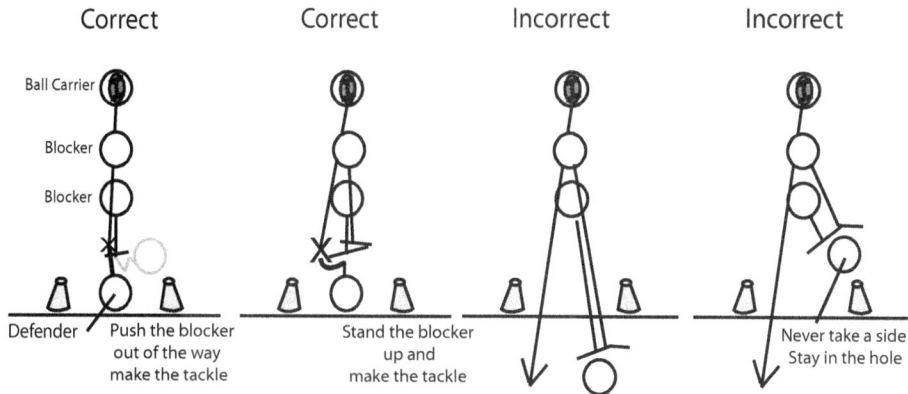

Two-on-one for defensive ends

This time put markers only on one side and leave the second side open.
The objective on this drill is to maintain containment on the runner. The
defensive end will stop the blocker or blockers and force the runner to the
inside or make the tackle. There is a lot more ground to protect on this
drill so you have to be sure what you want from your ends. I want him to
turn the runner in or force him deep into the backfield to give time for the
rest of the team to fill in from the inside. If he can make the tackle then
that is by far the first thing on his list of "to-do's".

You want to keep the outside leg back and away from the blockers so they
can't get you on the ground, use your inside shoulder to take on the block
and leave the outside open and away to cut off the outside and force the
runner back into the arms of the linemen and linebackers that are coming
from the inside out. This is where I will put my best and fastest defensive
player because there is not a lot of help out there on the ends and they will
have to make a lot of one-on-one tackles.

I will add more blockers and linebackers to this drill to give them a more
game like look and a feel for where the help is coming from.

Keep your outside leg back
and away from the blocker

Use your inside shoulder
to take on the block

Keep containment and/or force to the outside

If you want more contact put an additional marker on the
outside and make the runner stay inside the markers

Add blockers because you can

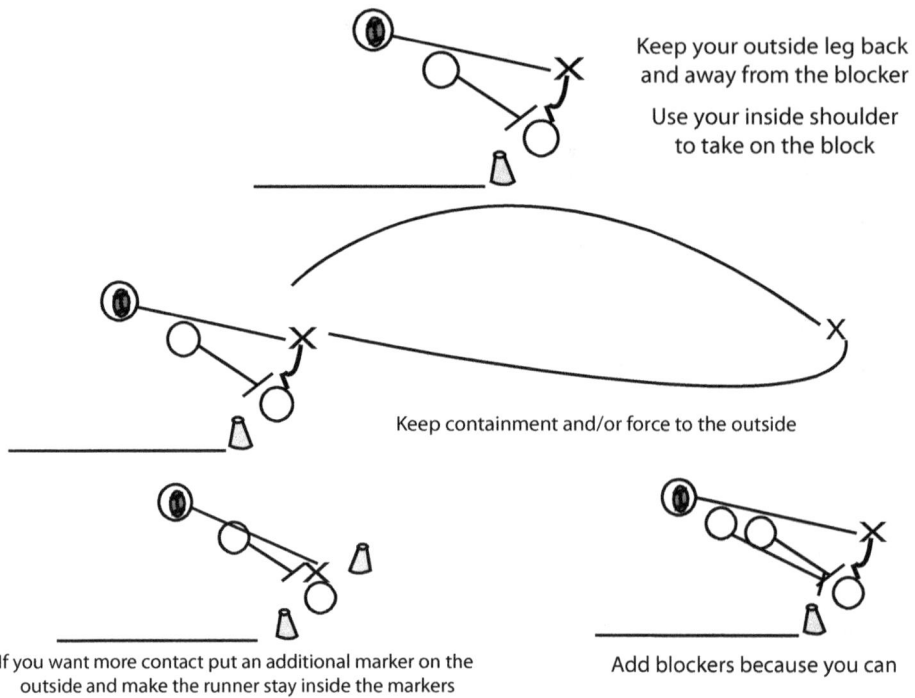

Two-on-one for the linemen

For the linemen's drill you can add additional linemen as a blocker on the
line and a fullback as the second blocker, then the runner. Also you can
put two linemen on the line as to simulate a double team block, either way
will work but when you go to the three-on-one and up I will start with
them already standing just the same as the rest of the teams drill.

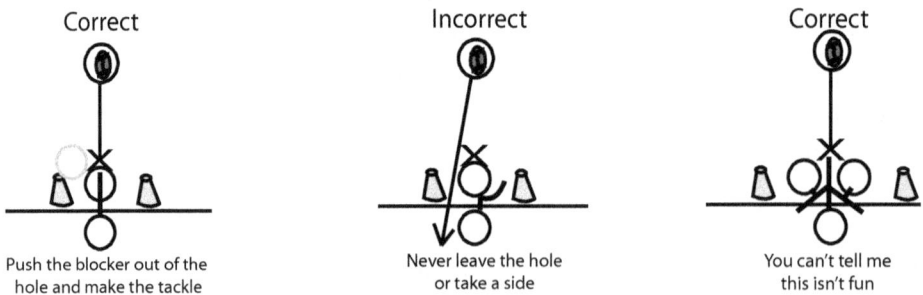

Correct

Incorrect

Correct

Push the blocker out of the
hole and make the tackle

Never leave the hole
or take a side

You can't tell me
this isn't fun

Split six blitz (linemen & linebackers)

This drill is just for the linemen and linebackers only and it is also specific to the split six defense. If you don't run the split six defense there is no need for this drill. But you should get an idea of how to set up your own drill that will help you design one that will reflect your defense.

Put down markers on the ground for the distance between the linemen that would be normal for your age group. Put your linemen down in a three-point stance with a linebacker directly behind him. On the snap of the ball the linemen takes the call side like right side inside means that the linemen will go to the inside or the side with the ball. The linebacker will take the outside or away from the ball. Be sure they don't over slant outside their area of responsibility. The linebacker is coming off the hip of the linemen just enough to get thru the line and into the backfield. You can also call it strong side and weak side if you want and if you have older players that can read the offensive line formations.

This drill should only take a few minutes to run with markers then you can add linemen to the offensive side to give a real game time look.

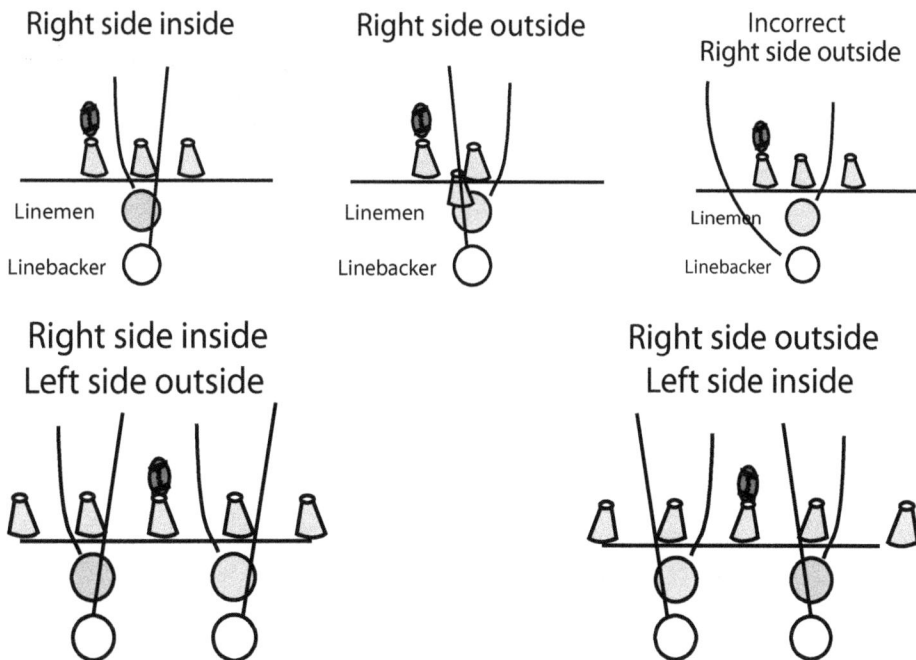

Right side inside

Right side outside

Incorrect
Right side outside

Linemen

Linebacker

Linemen

Linebacker

Linemen

Linebacker

Right side inside
Left side outside

Right side outside
Left side inside

Loops (defensive ends & outside linebackers)

On the loop the defensive ends now have inside responsibility and the outside goes to the linebackers. You set this up by putting markers down to simulate the offense and have the defensive end and outside linebackers run it to make sure they understand their area of responsibility. If you have a running back or whoever comes out of the backfield on the call side the outside responsibility man has him until he crosses the line of scrimmage.

Normal

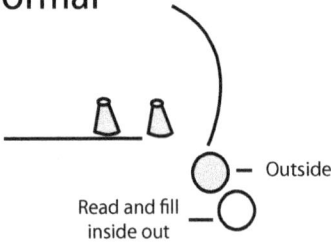

Read and fill inside out

Outside

Loop

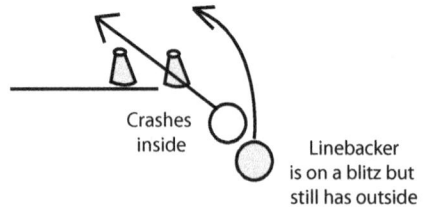

Crashes inside

Linebacker is on a blitz but still has outside

Normal

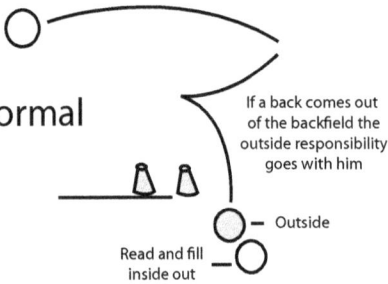

If a back comes out of the backfield the outside responsibility goes with him

Read and fill inside out

Outside

Loop

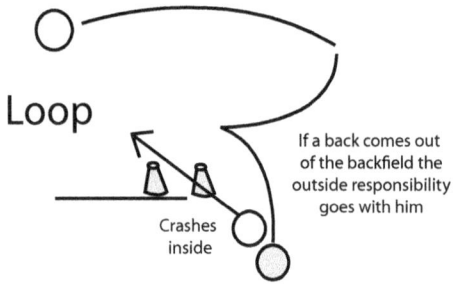

Crashes inside

If a back comes out of the backfield the outside responsibility goes with him

Sprint out or pass twenty-four (quarterbacks & receivers)
I run the sprint out offense so I set this drill up for the quarterbacks and
sometimes with receivers. First I set up some markers in a half circle to
show the quarterback where I want him to run. I will have no backfield
or receivers to start with but then bring them in later as we move thru the
drills. I include the snap with this drill to make sure he is getting the ball
correctly. The quarterback will put his hand under the center with a firm
amount of pressure to the center's butt. The reason for this is when you
get in a game and the center is running on a little adrenaline he will take
off a little early while hiking the ball. If the quarterback is not
putting enough pressure on the center's butt the ball will come up and hit
the quarterback in the face. If he is doing it right the quarterback's hand
will ride forward with the center and the ball will hit him in the hand.
Next the quarterback will take a big step to the backfield and start towards
the tailback which I use a marker at first. I want him to get deep before
he starts his route towards the line of scrimmage. Once he turns up field
this is where he must make his decision as to whether he will pass or run,
remember run first pass second. (Green means go.) I will set up either
receivers or markers for him to hit once he decides. You can also have
someone either rush him or drop back in coverage. I do not run this drill
every practice but when I see the quarterback getting lazy and not getting
deep enough or I just want to sharpen the route, I will bring it back into
practice.

You can give the QB a number of where
you want the pass to go before the
snap or you can yell it out
as he rounds the turn

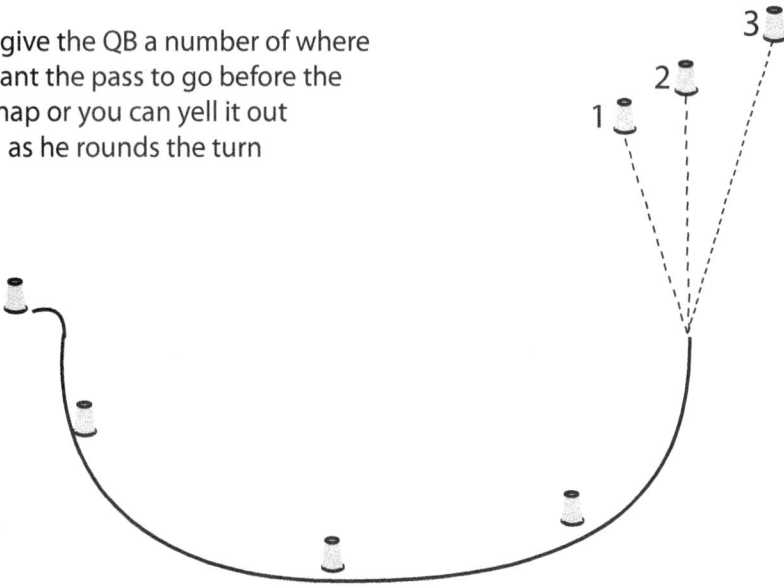

Make sure he is getting deep enough
before he turns up field so his
shoulders are facing forward
when he is ready to pass the ball

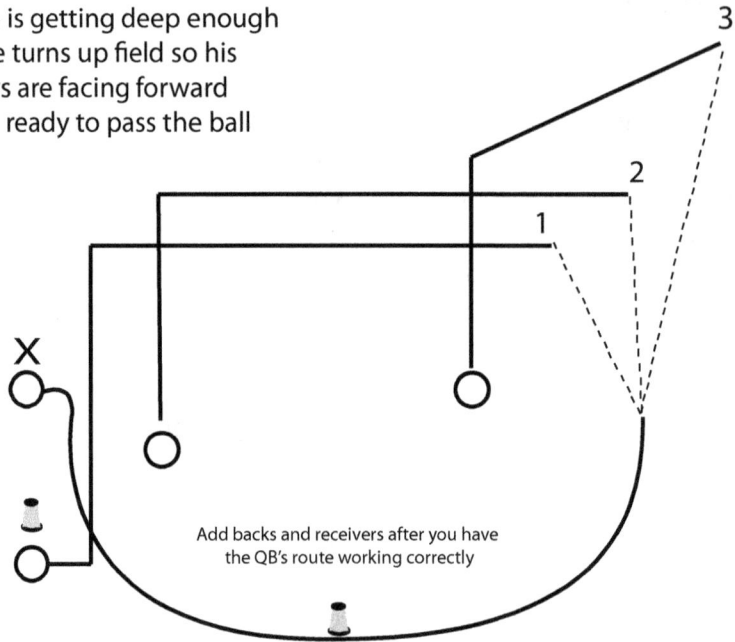

3

2

1

X

Add backs and receivers after you have
the QB's route working correctly

Passing techniques (quarterbacks & receivers)

A lot of coaches think that if you can throw the ball far you are a good quarterback, I do not feel this way. Sometimes a pass has to be laid right in over the linebacker's head or low and hard under the defensive backs reach whatever you think there are a few things to consider when throwing a pass.

One, on a slant pattern you need the ball to be low and hard. When I run this drill I have a receiver run the slant pattern and on the snap of the ball have the quarterback just stand up and throw the ball as quick as he can. There is no time to set your feet or look off the safety, who should be on the other side anyway. The slant is a very quick play, so run the drill that way.

Second is the loop pass, the quarterback will throw it over some other players or assistant coaches or I will sometimes take a quarterback over to where there are some obstacles that he can throw around, thru or over, swing sets, monkey bars, hallways whatever you can find. This will also help the receivers with their concentration.

The third is of course the long ball but it must be on target or what's the point?

An important side note is to make sure they are in full pads before you do the obstacle drills.

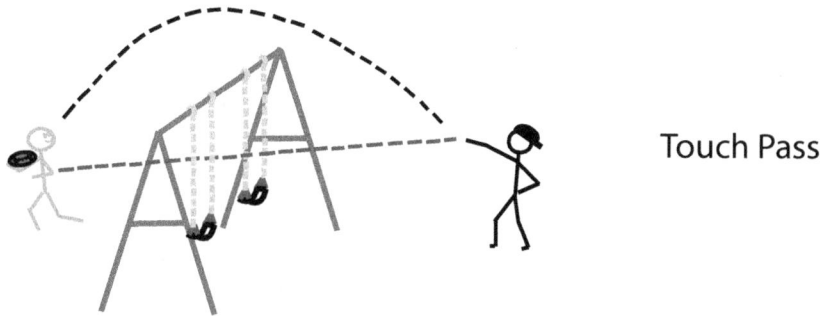

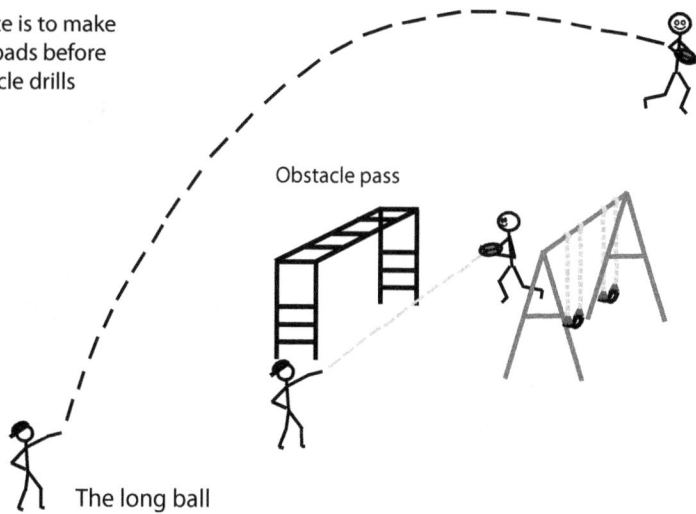

Low and Hard

Touch Pass

An important side note is to make sure they are in full pads before you do the obstacle drills

Obstacle pass

The long ball

Drop back pass (quarterbacks)

The linemen run past the quarterback but do not touch him at this point, you can add that later if you want, I never have. Line up three or four sets of linemen and have them rush the quarterback. There doesn't have to be any receivers at first just get him used to dropping back the right number of steps and throwing the ball. Later you can add the receivers as you feel the need.

I also added a scramble technique to the DVD because it was too hard to put into words and draw.

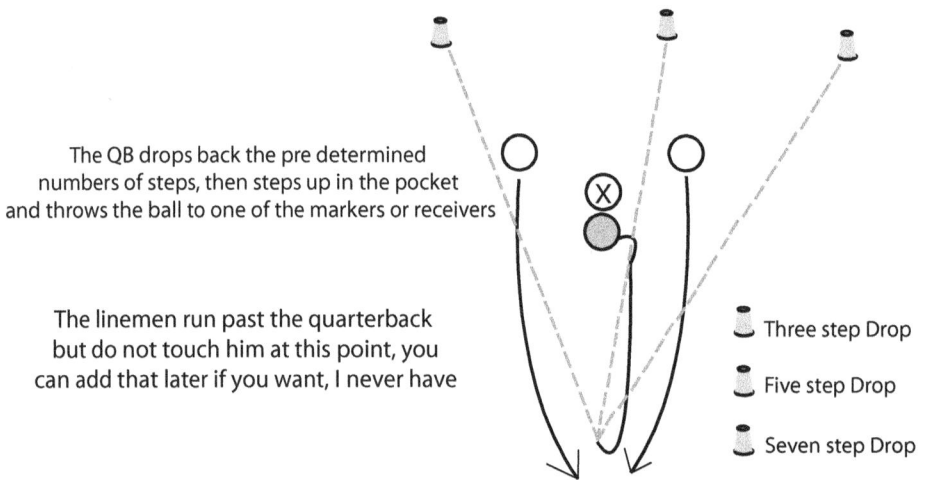

The QB drops back the pre determined numbers of steps, then steps up in the pocket and throws the ball to one of the markers or receivers

The linemen run past the quarterback but do not touch him at this point, you can add that later if you want, I never have

Three step Drop

Five step Drop

Seven step Drop

Passing on the run (quarterbacks & receivers)

Being able to pass on the run can be a big asset. Just have the quarterback and receiver run in the same direction and have the quarterback throw the ball while running towards the sidelines. They will soon realize that the ball will carry further as the momentum will cause it to sail in the direction of the run. After a short time they will make the adjustment to the pass.

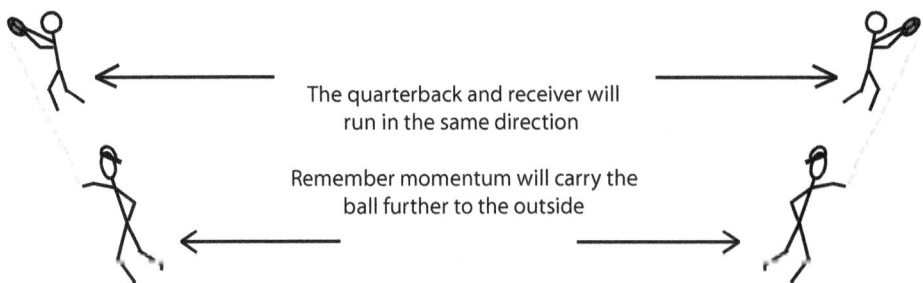

The quarterback and receiver will run in the same direction

Remember momentum will carry the ball further to the outside

Pump and go (quarterbacks & receivers)

Put a defender on your receivers and don't tell him what you are running, just alternate the plays with sideline patterns and slants. The receiver will wait to see if it is a pass or a fake. When the receiver sees what the quarterback is going to do then he will either catch the ball or turn up field. If the quarterback fakes the pass then the receiver will turn up field, if there is no fake then stay on your route. This is the rule unless I say different, anytime the quarterback fakes the pass, the receivers should turn up field. This is for two reasons; one is if the defensive back is too close to the receiver and the other is if the quarterback wants to run the ball. When the receiver turns up field the defensive back will follow him, if not then he will throw the ball and six points for us. So when you run this drill do it enough times that the receivers get used to watching for the ball or the fake.

An important side note is that if the receiver doesn't look at the quarterback when he does the fake, then the defensive back will not come up or as we say bite on the out pattern.

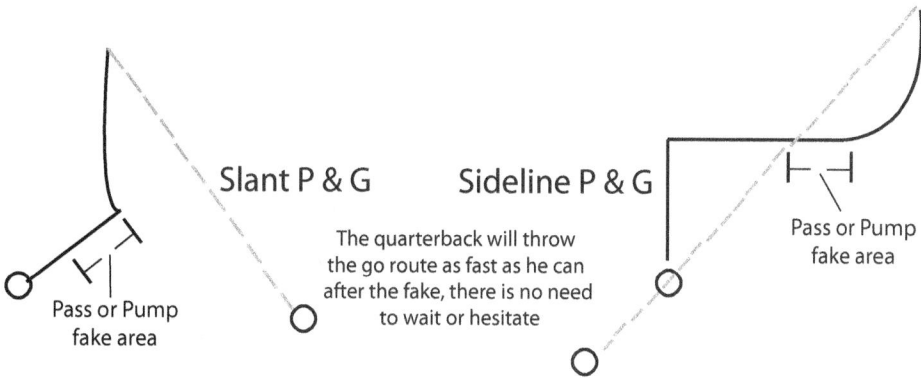

Slant P & G   Sideline P & G

The quarterback will throw
the go route as fast as he can
after the fake, there is no need
to wait or hesitate

Pass or Pump
fake area

Pass or Pump
fake area

Quick hands (receivers)

Put four or whatever amount you want in two lines about ten yards apart,
the ones without the ball turn their backs to the ones with the ball. The
ones with the ball will throw the pass and just before it gets to the receivers the coach will yell NOW! The receivers will then turn and try to make
the catch.

Passers   Receivers

After they pass the ball   When they have the ball
they become the receivers   then they become the passers

Hit and spin (running backs)

Put two tackling dummies in a line about five yards apart and have the
runner start about five yards back from the first tackling dummy. On the
snap of the ball have the runner go to the first dummy, hit it hard, spin off
it and go to the next one and do the same; after the last one have the runner
sprint to the markers or the goal line. I always give the runners a ball to
hang on to so they get used to having it their hands.

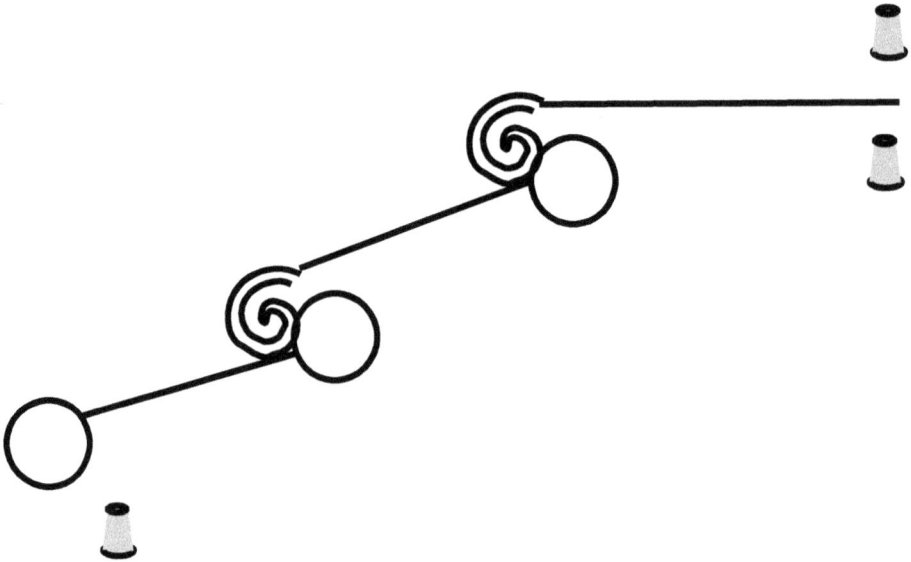

Pass gauntlet (receivers & backs)

Form two lines one for the receivers and one for the gauntlet, as with all drills they alternate lines after they do one or the other. The lines are facing each other about ten to fifteen yards apart. The receiving line will start running toward the gauntlet to catch the ball, try to put the ball just in front of the gauntlet. The gauntlet line cannot touch the receiver until he has the ball, then they hit him, but are not allowed to tackle the receiver. Their purpose is to try to knock the ball down or to loosen it from its rightful owner.

You can start out slow and soft and then increase the level of intensity as you feel the need and I do feel the need.

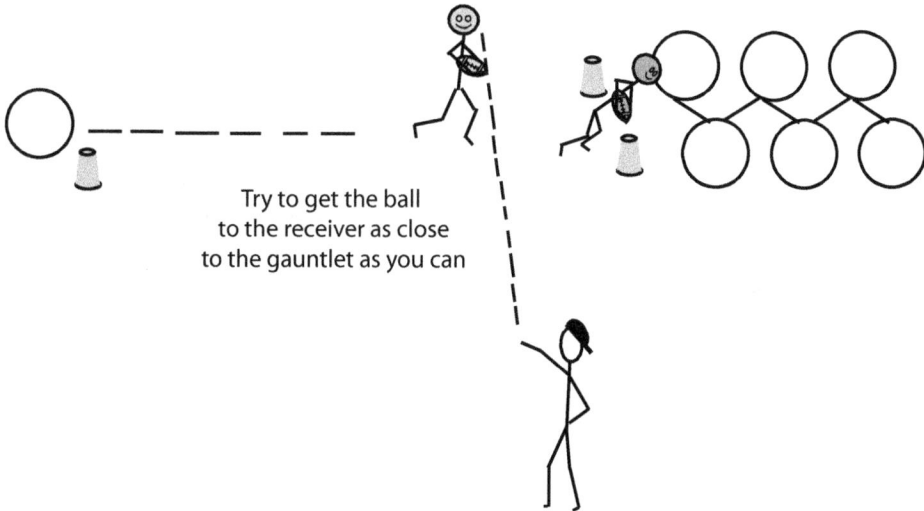

Try to get the ball
to the receiver as close
to the gauntlet as you can

Open field tackling (defensive backs, linebackers & defensive ends)
Same as the form tackling drill but you set the markers further apart
depending on the group you have. The only group that will not do this
is the linemen, theirs is from the three-point stance and with a blocker in
their face. The rest is in a running mode towards each other at a slight
angle right or left, but only the runner knows which way he will cut. The
runner has to wait till he gets to the second marker before he can make
his cut. The tackler is running to the same mark but breaks down his feet
just before the ball carrier makes his cut then he chooses his angle and
proceeds to the tackle. As they improve you will move the markers further
apart to make it more difficult.

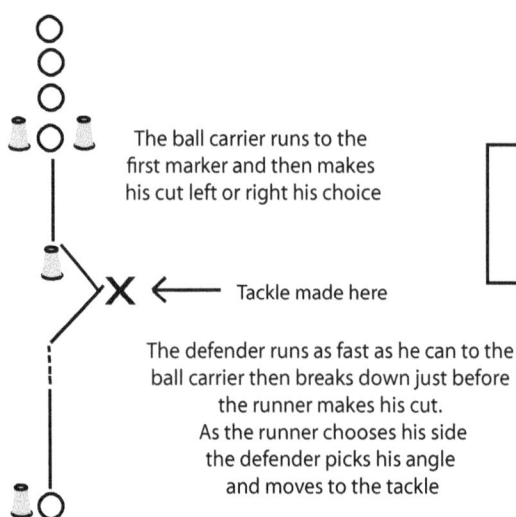

The ball carrier runs to the
first marker and then makes
his cut left or right his choice

This is a very hard drill for the
younger ages but it will become
easier the more you do it

Tackle made here

The defender runs as fast as he can to the
ball carrier then breaks down just before
the runner makes his cut.
As the runner chooses his side
the defender picks his angle
and moves to the tackle

Zone (defensive backs & linebackers)
I take the linebackers and the defensive backs and set them up in regular
split six formation. At the snap of the ball they drop back in their zones.
I will try to expose their weaknesses by throwing the ball where they are
not. They will try to get to that spot before the ball touches the ground.
After I see they can get to their zone ok I will add the receivers to the
drill and start over with patterns. There are no defensive linemen at this
point so I have plenty of time to make the throw. I will let the quarterback
throw a few if they are good enough or in other words older.

If you have a lot of players then I rotate them in after each set of plays, but I don't rotate them in one-by-one only as a set like the first team, second team and so on down the line.

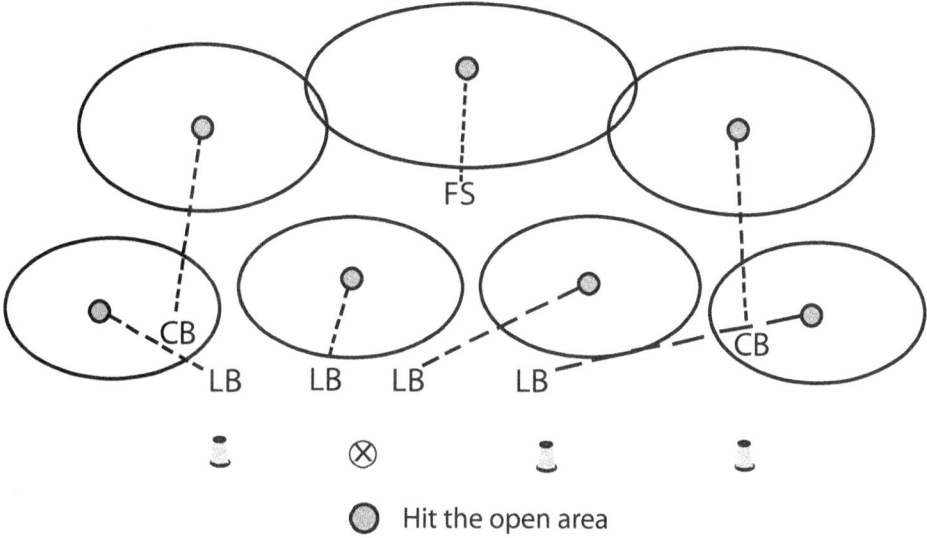

FS

CB LB LB LB LB CB

⊗

🔵 Hit the open area

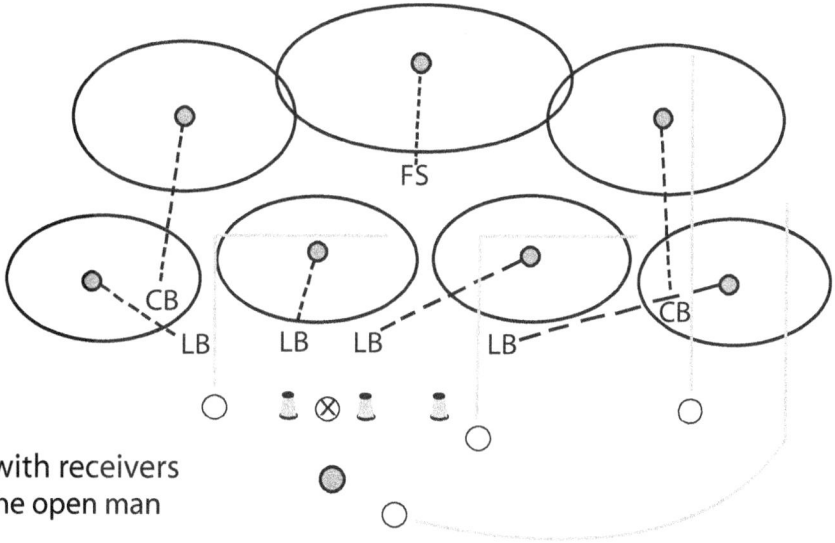

FS

CB LB LB LB LB CB

⊗

Zone with receivers
  Hit the open man

Interception drill (defensive ends, defensive backs & linebackers)
You never want to wait for the ball to get to you. Always and there is no
exception always try to get the ball at its highest point. The way we
practice this is with the interception drill. Line up about fifteen yards
away from the ball facing the quarterback. The player runs towards the
quarterback and the quarterback or I will throw the ball high and at an
angle left or right at the edge of the oncoming players ability. The player
will try to reach up and catch the ball at the highest point possible. Never
wait for the ball to come to you.

The receiver will run towards the
QB, then make his cut after he sees
which way the ball is thrown

fifteen to twenty
yards apart

There are a number of ways to throw the ball
I like the high and away, but you can use the
right at their gut or numbers or whatever.
The main thing is to make it hard for the receiver

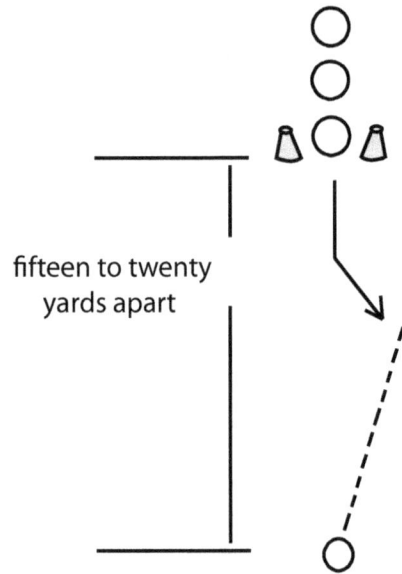

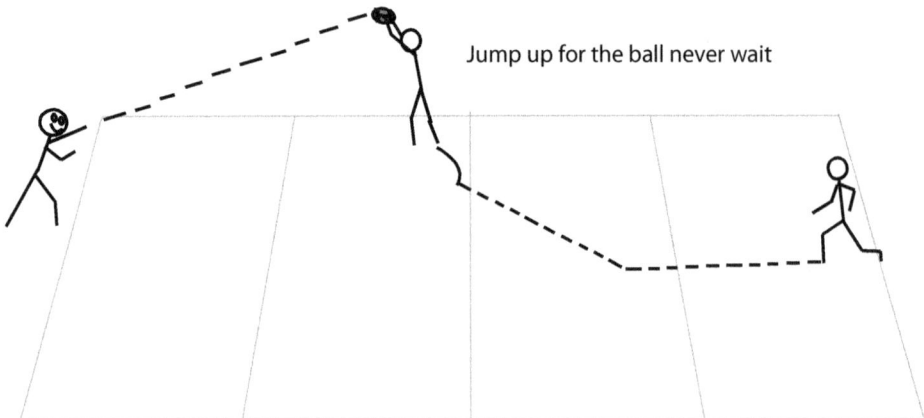

Jump up for the ball never wait

Receiving technique pinkies and thumbs (general)
The technique for catching the ball is the same for all, thumbs together above your waist pinkies together below the waist.

Thumbs together above you waist

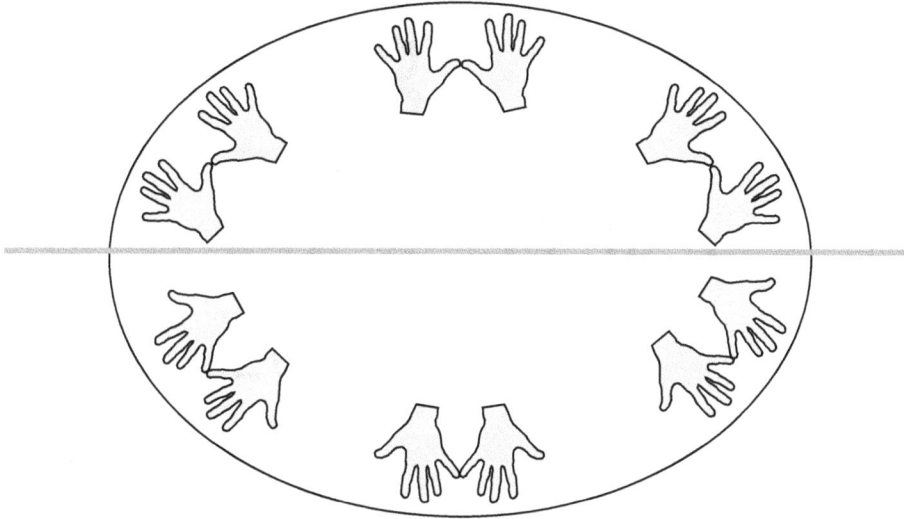

Pinkies together below the waist

Goal line four-on-four
I make a small area with tackling dummies or markers just a little smaller than normal and I use anywhere from four on up to a full team on this drill. The most fun is four-on-four in a very small place. Set up markers with just enough room for a runner to get thru. Put two down linemen on offense, two on defense, two linebackers, one runner and one lead blocker so now you have four-on-four. Give the plays to the offense which is basically left, right or middle, then let the defense just run regular. Later I will add some defensive calls to help liven things up.

They must not go outside the markers. I have two teams with the losers running or doing a lot of push-ups. One point is awarded after every time the runner gets to the pre-determined goal line or if the defense can stop him. Everyone has to have a turn in their positions. The last two attempts can be with their best of the best. (Receivers are runners and defensive backs are linebackers.) Both sides get five on defense and five on offense. Let the games begin. This is an intense drill but it will build team unity and a real need to win. Always mix up the teams so that every time you run it there will be different players on the two sides. I will not let the quarterback in on this drill unless he is also on defense and wants to.

I hope this gives you a good idea on how to set up a drill and how to make it look like your program. You want to design some more that will be closer to what you want to run, if you run a wishbone then have drills that teach to read and toss the ball to the runners. If you pass a lot run more passing drills and quarterback drills that reflect your system. Most of all have fun, if you are having fun then the team will as well.

Chapter Six
First Day with Your Team

I guess the first thing you need to know is how did you get your team? Was it assigned to you? Did you pick them from a field of many or did you inherit them from a coach that couldn't get a win? I love that one the most it's less pressure on you and a lot more satisfying to turn a team around and make them winners. Since that is the most fun and probably the most challenging let's approach this first day as though that is the task. Everybody wants to win so the principles remain the same. On the first day I gather the team around and introduce my coaching staff and myself. I start with a speech that goes something like this. " I love football. I love everything about football, the smell of the grass, the cool fall air, the sound of pads hitting. That long pass for a touchdown to win the game. I have been involved with football for over 38 years, 22 of them coaching and 19 as a head coach. I have been very fortunate to be with a lot of winning programs. I love to win and I can tell you that winning is a lot more fun than losing. I can tell you I win a lot. I have taken many teams from never winning a game to going on to an undefeated year. I promise you if you do what I tell you to do and trust me and come together as a team, we will not only have a lot of fun; we will have a lot of victories. I know that, and I want you to know that, so for now lean on me.

When you see it come together in practice and after the first game, when we have our first win. I want you to have your own winning attitude and project that to everyone you meet, so that when they look at you, they will not have to ask if you won your game they will know, they will see it your eyes because being a winner is something you just can't hide. These coaches you see behind me are dedicated to you and the team's success, together we can build a team that we all can be proud of. Who's with me? Now get up and run as fast as you can and get me a leaf off that tree over there."

Even though I love to hear myself talk, a pep talk can only go so far. Coach Bo Schembechler the great coach from Michigan in the book, The

Football Coaching Bible writes, "Team meetings and pre-game pep talks are overrated. I prefer one-on-one relationships. They provide the opportunity to establish trust on both sides."

One of the first things I try to do is instill in my entire program the importance of being honest in all aspects of the game. You can't expect others to be honest with you unless you are first honest with them. Bo goes on further in the same book to say that, "Honesty is the core of coaching." Be honest with them from the very beginning and that will build trust between you and everyone involved in your program. It may be hard at first, but stay with it and in the long run you and everyone will be a lot happier and have a lot more fun.

I could go on about trust all day but for more, go get the book The Football Coaching Bible or rent it from the library and read the entire chapter on Inner Drive and Motivation by Bo Schembechler. He puts a fine point on it and tells you why it will help you bring your program to a higher level. For now the point is you want to start off on the right foot with a positive outlook and a good feeling about you, your staff and your team. Now let's get to work.

I will always ask them what they want to achieve this year, like do you want the league championship, state championship or be undefeated whatever it is. Then we set goals for the year and I go over with them what I expect and what it will take to achieve the goals we set. Now that you have gone over the basics and laid down a foundation you are ready to get started.

Conditioning

Conditioning is very important; you want to first warm them up with a run or some other low impact exercise. Then have them start their stretches. If you don't know any it is always a good idea to check with a local trainer, school P.E. department and/or Internet.

Most of the time I will supervise the stretch at first to insure they don't hurt themselves by doing some stretch that was deemed unsafe ten years ago. Now that you have them warmed up you are ready to do the standard exercises that you did when you were in school. Jumping jacks, cotton-picker's, push-ups, etc. This part of the practice will be the same from now till the end of the season, so set up a routine with some players to lead them. At first if you don't know this team that well, pick a few and then rotate them till you have some team captains or quarterbacks and linebackers. As soon as I know whom I want to call the plays on the field I will use them. Most of the time it is the quarterbacks and the linebackers, I want the team to get used to hearing their voices and taking their commands.

Most football leagues do not allow hitting at first but that doesn't slow me down, there is a lot of stuff you can do before the hitting starts. One is to set up the offense and start running plays, getting down the timing and spacing. There are also a lot of drills that will help get the team ready for the first day in pads. In the drill sections I broke down the drills to hitting and non-hitting, this will be a good time to run your non-hitting ones. Find the ones that go with your program and set up a routine they can do now and when you have them in pads. Then all you have to do is make a few adjustments later to allow contact.

The first thing I will do is start separating the field into positions so the assistant coaches can start working with their groups. In the younger ages there will always be a lot of quarterbacks to start with, it is your job to start moving them into the position that will work best for them as well as for the team. I don't force any player into any position they don't want, I will sell them on why they want to be where they will do the most good and have the most fun.

In the older ages you will have players that have been playing a position for a number of years so the field will separate themselves for the most part, but there are always a few that would do better in a different spot. Steve Young was a defensive back when he got to BYU, then moved to quarterback and later became MVP in the Super Bowl. There is an art and/or a gift to recognizing talent and being able to utilize it to the benefit of your players and your team.

The one thing to remember at this point is that you are not in pads yet and things will change so don't make any big time commitments just yet, but don't be afraid either just move forward and start working kids into positions and tell them that, "I just want to get a look at you in that spot so just consider it for now and we can make changes after we get some pads on." This will give them a feel for that spot and after you do a little selling they may want to stay. Selling that spot is easy if you take the high road and use the positive approach, "I think that spot works for you and I have some plays I will show you later that I think you will be great for." Try to be as truthful as you can. I want him there but if he doesn't want to be there then move on and find someone else.

Now that you have a good start on positions you can run some drills and start pulling groups together and run a few plays. I always start with offense because it will take about twice as long as defense and you can't hit yet anyway so it is easy to do offense to begin.

I start with my number one play the twenty-four. I try to get them to understand the concept and how we will progress from there into a lot of plays that will start with the twenty-four. The timing and the spacing are general at this point because there are no pads and no hitting. That will change a little when you can hit so for now I just want to set the foundation.

By the time we are in pads we will have a great start on offense and have a little defense set up so it will make it a lot easier to make a few adjustments to those plays and add some more when we are in the full practice mode.

Later I will use the ten perfect plays after practice, but for now I will run because for the most part the kids have been laying around all summer and need to get their bodies back into football shape. That will take sometime, about a week of hard practice.

Getting to know your players

As you get to know your team some will rise to the top, but beware they are not in pads yet. There will always be some that look good at first but lose ground when the hitting starts. Then there are those that seem to be waiting, then wake up when they hear the sound of pads crashing.

A secret I was not sure I wanted to share with you is something I do with my teams that I find gives me more information on players in one day then you may get in a whole season. If you are healthy enough and willing what I do is put together a little game just like the one you would do on Thanksgiving, more popularly knows as the Turkey Bowl. I play a game with the team, no pads, no helmet just a little pick up game. I pick the two leaders and then I let them pick the players and that includes me and whatever willing assistant coaches. You can find out more in that game than weeks of practice. You will see who the leaders are, the ball hogs, the ones that can't shut up in the huddle and the ones that will do anything to win. I try to be the quarterback at first then give a few of the kids a shot at it. Most of the time they know each other because they have played together for years in all kinds of situations like school and other teams, baseball, basketball, etc. they will know who are the players and who's not.

An important side note here is to be careful, sometimes they will not give a kid a chance because they may not know him very well or he hasn't been given a fair chance in the past, so try to involve everyone so they all have a shot at being the best they can be.

Now that you survived that, if you survived that, then you will be able to start to put your team together. The first thing I like to do is get the field of ten quarterbacks down to two or three. Most of the time the second and third quarterback is too good to sit on the bench waiting. I like to put him in another spot if I can, but in the older ages you have a lot of kids so you may want to leave him as a true back up. In high school and older you will have under classmen to work with so bringing one along as a back up and getting him in the game as the situation allows is always a good idea.

Once I have a quarterback or two I start to throw some passes. It is a great way to get everybody running and a good way to start to find who you want where. As far as linemen go, the pick up game is also a quick way to find them. They can't catch, run, or throw the ball so the line coach can find them quickly.

As you find the players you want in certain positions you will break them off the main pack and send them with the appropriate coaches. They can define the drills that best suit that position.

Very shortly you will see players you want to play in a particular position but they may not want to go. This is the hardest and the most fun for me. I want to put a player in the best spot not only for me but for him. It seems like every year the first one I try to move is the tight end. Most of the time in their past the tight end has always been a linemen and they see that as a blocking position so they don't understand that for me the tight end is one of the most important players on the field. I use him in very important downs and distance situations and in my system he is the one that does a lot of scoring. So that is how I sell the position not as a linemen, but as a receiver hiding on the line for big plays, in big games, on big downs. "Can you handle that son?" That is just one example of many, you will want to examine that approach a little because I have seen coaches just tell a player, "No, you are not a quarterback, you are a running back so just do it or go sit on the bench." I would say that this type of approach is just a little too, what's the word I'm looking for, oh yeah, dumb. You don't want a disgruntled quarterback running the ball, but a happy running back/back up quarterback running the ball. So my advice to you is don't force a player into a position, show him why he would want to be there and how it will help the team and himself.

When you go to build a house you don't ask the plumber to do the framing or the cement guys to do the electric work, you want the right guy for the job for every position. Try to recognize the talent and put it where it belongs. If you have a player that doesn't care that he will be number two or three but wants to be the running back anyway that is fine I don't have a problem with that. I give him the chance to be a starter, but he is comfortable being a back up. There is usually a reason for that. Maybe his dad was that position, maybe he likes a player on a pro-team or maybe he really doesn't want to be a starter. Maybe he is only there because his parents want him there and he is ok with playing just enough for daddy to say, "good job son". Maybe, and my favorite, "I just like to be with my friends." They will never tell you any of that so you will just have to get a feel for it and do what's best for the kids.

Position management

Finding the right guy for the job is hard but fun. I love to see kids do well in a spot they didn't think was right for them, but later come to realize that it is. I want to go through a little position finding drill just to give you a starting point, but don't get crazy about it just try to see how I came up with it and work it from there. First of all my best quarterback I ever had was also the top seed tennis player in the state at twelve years old. Most good football players are also great athletes in sports other than football. So just because he may be a good baseball player doesn't mean he can't be good at football. I look for the right guy for the job and not always the ones that think they are the best player for that position.

Let's start with the **quarterback**. He should be someone with natural leadership abilities and a true team player, unselfish, smart and confident without being arrogant. He should be strong-minded and able to have others want to follow him. Next the running backs, first the **three back** or what I like to think of him as the blocking back. This is a hard spot to fill because he carries the ball only a few times during a game and mostly to set up another play. He should be as big as he can with the ability to hang onto the ball and gain a few yards. The **two back** should be one of the fastest players on offense, it's always great if he is a great runner, but that is not always going to happen you have to take what you get unless you can recruit. Size is not as big a factor as some would like you to believe. My best runner was the smallest two back I ever had, he went on to become one of the best three point shooters for his high school basketball team. He was one of the shortest players they ever had on the team and still started for them for two years. He was just a great athlete. So the two back should also be a strong fearless player not caring about the size of the other team. The **four back** or slot back should be fast and a good receiver, he should also be a good blocker because he will be blocking at least half the time with the other half in pass patterns. This is also someone that can catch the ball in traffic. The **wide receiver** should be the fastest or at least one of the fastest players on the team. I would like him to be tall but that is not the only deciding factor. Being able to run the pattern right and catch the ball is the most important thing to consider. The **tight end** is the hardest position to fill because he has to be everything to everybody. He must be able to block, run fast, catch the ball and look like a linemen all at the same time. I try to get the biggest kid I can that can catch the ball. I think this is standard in football, most tight ends are big strong receivers. The **linemen** are the ones that need to be big but I think big is a little overrated. I love big tall linemen but I will never turn away a kid that can block well and run fast. You can always use a little smaller linemen as the pulling guard and leave the real big guys as tackles and centers.

I should have started with defense because this is where I put the best of the best. This time I want to start with the **defensive linemen**, they should be big, fast, quick and strong but I want to say that I don't care that much about the size although that is a big factor especially when you come up against big front line, however being able to shed the block and make the tackle is far more important than how big he is. So I want linemen who can move and get to the ball carrier from sideline to sideline and bring him down. Next are the **linebackers** in the middle they have to be able to get inside the big guys and make a tackle in traffic. They need to be big, fast, strong and tough. They are the toughest kids you have with no apparent fear of death. I don't know about the death thing but they should be fearless. The **outside linebackers** should be the same as the inside line-backers with the exception of being able to move faster to the outside. Possessing all the traits of the inside linebackers with the ability to move laterally quickly. That brings us to the **defensive ends** they have to be the very best players you have, they have to be able to stand inside and take on the blocks of the offensive linemen and pulling guards as well as being able to stop the outside plays. They have to make tackles in traffic as well as open field on an end around or sweeps. Sometimes they are the last guys before the secondary and that could be the difference between a first down or touchdown. The **defensive backs** are the fastest players as well with the ability to run backwards almost as fast as they run forwards. They also need to be able to make a play on the ball and/or catch it in all types of athletic positions. The **safety** is the last line of defense with the ability to move in all directions and also run backwards as fast as he can forwards. I like to have a tall safety with great hands and great field presents. He needs to know where he is on the field in relationship to all the offensive receivers. He must be fast to make up any ground that might occur when the runners and receivers get loose from the pack.

This is just the basics to get you started. Depending on your program you will need to find the kids that suit the plays you run.

Parents and all that

A quick word about parents. I think if you set up a few rules at the beginning of the season you will cut down on trouble during the season. I will set up a meeting for the parents at the earliest opportunity and go over what I expect from them and what they can expect from me. I give them a practice and game schedule laying out the year. I tell them that it's my way or the highway. I try to give them a feel that I know what I'm doing. I tell them if they have a question they can read my book first then if they still have questions then come to me after or before practice and I will tell them why I did that. That way I sell another book and by the time they are done reading it the season is over. Just kidding. (I mean about the season being over before they get done with my book.) I tell them that their job is to support the team and the kids. I also throw in a little speech about being a good sport and that means not yelling at the referees. When the kids see their parents making fools of themselves and getting nowhere with the referees that only hurts the team. I am the one who will bring up any discrepancies with the officiating, that is my job and I take it very serious. There will almost always be the parent that is smarter, bigger, and a lot dumber than you, who wants to run your program from the stands. Let him but as soon as he comes out of the stands you need to be ready to put him back. I take a strong position on this issue and I have no patience for parents that get in my face and want me to do something different. I tell them I am here for the kids and not for them. Everybody on my team plays and everybody has fun. If you don't like the way I coach and you think you can do better then go tell the athletic director or president and get your own team. I will also tell parents that I donate hours of my time to the kids and yes my boy will play every down on every team and if you don't like it you can get your own team and have your boy start every play. On a more general term every parent thinks their kid is the best player on the field and sometimes that's true but the ones that say that are usually the ones that are wrong. If he is the best player then you will have no trouble seeing it for yourself and they wouldn't have to come tell you. To avoid all this you will find that if you stick to the meeting at the first of the year and lay down a set of rules or guidelines you will not have that extreme of a problem later. Let them know they can come talk to you anytime and voice any concerns they may have. If you just tell them yes I do have only two down linemen but as you can see they still haven't scored on us and this is the third game. I can change the defensive now if you like, but the kids have kind of gotten use to it and listening to parents and changing things in the middle of the season has never really worked out for me. So I think we will just stick to what worked for me over the past twenty years. I am always nice, at first, but don't make me mad or I will promote your kid to water boy. Just kidding, **I never punish the kids because of their parents**. Through the years I have only had a few parents I needed protection from but only a few and for the most part they will understand after they see the team having fun and getting along. The key is to be upfront and honest with them and try to get them to see that it is for the kids and not for them.

Chapter Seven
First Day in Pads

You have to love the first day in pads, to me that is when football starts but be careful and start slow. You may have a tendency to want to see who the men and girls are, but you don't want to kill them on the first day. Start slow and build, you want to get them used to hitting and being hit. Try to praise good hits but don't put down bad ones, at least not yet. You may have some kids where this is there first time in a real football situation and they will need some time to love the hitting as much as you do. If you go too fast you will lose some kids and maybe not get them back. You can always kick it up a notch later but you don't want to get anybody hurt on their first day.

Now that you started hitting you will see a new team emerge and what fun that is. The drills become more game like and the plays have real meaning. Now you can start to put players in their permanent positions and start a depth chart. Here is one you can look at but I have seen so many different ones that you will probably make your own as soon as you can. You will need one soon, so I would set one up as soon as you can even before you get your team. I did mine so I could change it often, things happen, kids get hurt others will shine later, some need to get used to your program, some just quit, and still some will not be as good as you first thought. (Use a pencil.)

Bryant
Howard

◯

◯ ◯ ◯ ◯ ◯ ◯ ◯
Bean Davis Gardner ◯ Steed Franks Bills
Cline Mitchell Bower Scott Niel Bringhurst Smith
Bills

◯
Murri
Johnson

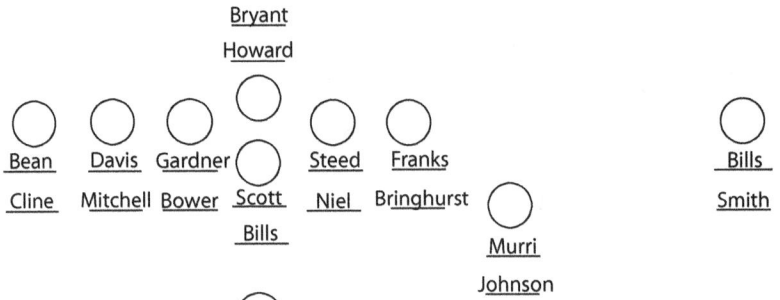

You can make it as deep as
you need to, depending on
how many kids you have

◯
Parr
Peterson

◯
Nappi
Roberts

DE   /\   /\   DE
Bean   Gardner   Steed   Franks
Cline Bower   Niel   Bringhurst

LOB   ROLB
Parr   Bryant
Peterson   LB   RB   Howard
            Bills   Nappi
            Mitchell Scott

LC   RC
Murri   Bills
Johnson   Smith

                S
              Davis
              Roberts

130

Offensives days

On the first day in pads for the offense you will start the same with warm ups and stretches. Then break into offensives groups, linemen, running backs, receivers and quarterbacks. Giving individual attention to each group to improving their skills for that position and go over plays you will be working on for that day. Offensive days will also be the time you want to break down the drills to give them the basic techniques of that position. For example you can show them the proper way to run a pass pattern or how to hold the ball or even how to hold their hands to catch the ball, a very important detail you don't want to take for granted. I am always surprised to see that no matter where I coach and at what level, I have kids that have never been taught the basic principles of football. If I could tell you one thing that is the most important that would be, **teach the basics**. A lot of coaches think they don't have the time but I will say that running the play right is great but if you can't make the catch or the tackle at the end of that play what good is it? A lot of the drills are designed to teach the proper way to tackle or catch or whatever; as you go thru this book and the DVD make sure you pay attention to the details of the drill to pick out the little things that make it work.

Individual position practice is also the time to show them how you want them to perform in their position for instance, the line coach can show a particular blocking technique that will be used for a play you run all season. Like for me how I want them to block on the twenty-four or twenty-eight power. Spend time where it will do the most good and don't waste time on stuff you don't have in your program. I never use drop back pass blocking. I always have them fire out on almost every play so teaching them to pass block is not always the best use of time. This time is for drills that are designed specifically for that position and for the offense you run. The same goes for the rest of the team, running backs, receivers, backs, and quarterbacks or however you break it down. Spend the time here to perfect their position and let them know what is expected of them there.

When you are working with just the quarterbacks this is the time to show them the details of how you want the play to be run. The little things are the most important. How they are to make their first step out on a twenty-four or hand position on the hand off. The way you move your feet so you are able to ride the running back on the pass thirty-three tight end delay. These are all very important details and need to be shown and worked on so when you bring them all together they will look like they know what they are doing.

While I'm working with the quarterbacks I will sometimes trade for a receiver or a running back with their groups so they have someone to throw the ball or hand it off to. Then I will trade them back about half way thru the drill. This will give the quarterbacks more reps and someone to throw to. Same with the receivers I give them a quarterback so they have someone to throw the ball. This gives the quarterbacks and receivers some reps together and a chance to work on plays and pass routes.

After the time for those drills is over I will pull the backs and receivers together without linemen and without any defense to make sure they can run the play the way I want with just the two groups. As we run this drill together with the backs and receivers I will watch the quarterbacks as the receiver and back coaches watch their respective positions. This will help with the timing of the play and give the player a chance to see the rest of the play in action. Last I will bring the linemen over and run it all again to see if everybody is on the same page. Whenever the team can run the plays right without defense I will add some defensive backs and linebackers as needed.

I always put the defensive linemen in last because they will put pressure on the play and I want the rest of the team to see it work smooth first, then we can make adjustments to it as the defensive linemen get jiggy with it.

One of the last drills I run towards the end of practice is the two-minute drill, then ten perfect plays. They are fast paced drills with a lot of running and hustling. This is a lot more training and learning than if you just ran sprints or ladders.

The two-minute drill is in chapter eight, you can go over it now or wait till you get to that chapter and review then to see more on how it is run. The ten perfect plays is a very important drill that brings awareness to the fact that execution is of the utmost importance and that it is not just a side note. Execution is the difference between failure and success. The difference between winning and losing can be as little as an inch or one dropped pass or one missed tackle. Run it right, run it perfect.

Defensive days

All this is the same for defensive days with just a few adjustments. I will always have tackling drills on every day with the exception of practices just before a game. I will go over that in the chapter on "First Game" and show you some of the important details of getting ready for a game but for now let's go over a few of the differences for defensive days and offensive days.

Starting with your warm ups, team stretch and conditioning, they will stay the same as always. On a defensive day, first of all there are a lot more tackling drills in as close to game type situation as possible. Then breaking into individual position drills using drills that are specific to defense (see DVD). Next break them apart in specific groups and then back together in groups till you have the team all together. When I bring them all back together I will use the offense to set up the defense so they can react to a play. (If you are getting ready for a team you will want to run their offense as close to that as you can with your scout team.) Remember that it is a defensive day and the focus has to remain on defense. However if your defense is ahead of the offense or the other way around you can make a change and work on one of them more. If I had a chance to scout a team I will take an 8.5 by 11 inch cardstock and print up the plays the other team is running. I use them with the scout team by holding them up in a huddle and each player looks at his position and follows the card.

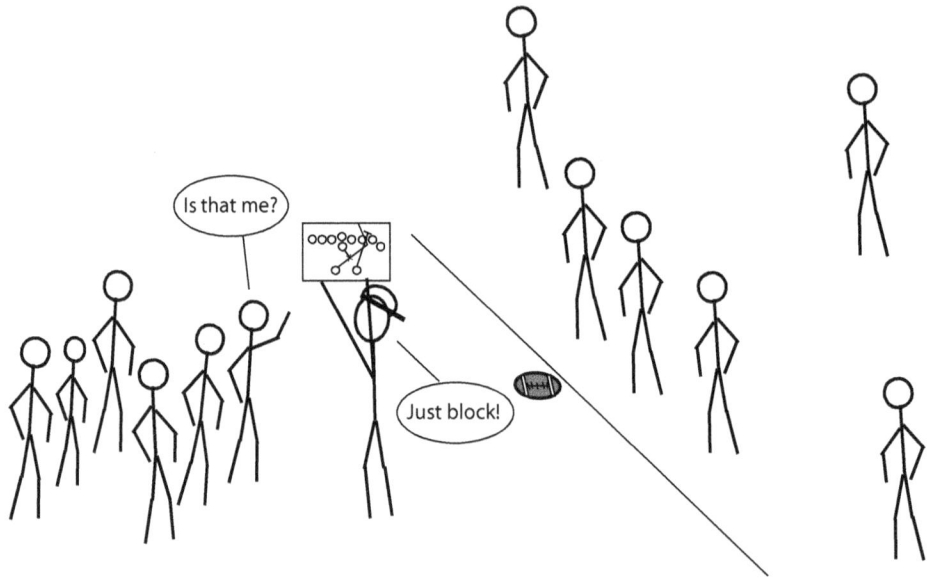

The scout team will look at the card and run their position, this will help the defense to see how the other team may look on Saturday. Just a short note, I have to say this again because I think it is so important. Teach the basics, this comes in to play more on defense than any other team. I've seen players from college and even pro put their heads down when going for a tackle. I know of no good coach that would ever tell a player that putting your head down and tackling with your eyes closed will work. Stay on your feet keep your head up and drive thru the ball carrier. Seems so simple but I still see it done wrong on every level, so to drive the point home one more time. **Teach the basics.**

You do the same on defensives days as you do on offensive days. First separating them into individual drills and then by bring them back together piece by piece until you have the whole team together again. Then run the defense as close to real time as you can with full speed and full contact hitting. Then end your practice with ten perfect plays on defense with all your different blitzes and pass coverage. If they run them perfect then great, if not start over. I like to run pass coverage when I can with me as quarterback. I send receivers out in patterns or just have them drop back into coverage and I try to hit the hole with them running to the ball. If all goes well then they are done, if not then we run.

Chapter Eight
What You Need to Know

All of the plays and formations in this book should be looked at like tools in your toolbox. You may not need every tool for every game but when you need a particular tool it sure feels good to know it's in the box clean, sharp and ready to use. Some of the things you will need in your toolbox that are very important and missing in a lot of other coaches programs are, the quick kick, safety for offense, slowing down a defense, two-minute offense and prevent defense. If I missed any and you see it on TV write it down and save it for when you need it, but for now let's look at these plays and how to use them.

1. **Quick kick**
2. **Safety, for offense**
3. **How to slow down the defense**
4. **Two-minute offense**
5. **Prevent defense**

Quick kick

The quick kick is used to gain field position (See chapter three for formation). I use it sparingly, but I have turned around momentum in a game on more than one occasion.

The when and where are the most important with this play. For those of you that haven't heard of a quick kick it is a punt run from a regular formation as to hide it from the defense till it is too late for them to set up a return. It is meant to have no possibility for a return and a long roll in your favor. It is mostly run on third down and long however that is not the only time I've seen it run. Sometimes on third and whatever but you are pinned down in your own end of the field and the defense is coming hard. This is the time I use it most but I have used it once to pin a team back when I was ahead by a lot and I just wanted them to have a long field to work with, to eat up more time. Whatever the case you make the call but don't forget you have it.

Safety

I'm pretty sure you all have heard of a safety, but I bet not as a play from scrimmage. I won a very big game with this play. What! You say? Let me explain. It was third and long from my five-yard line, I was up by six points, a touchdown and extra point for them, would be a loss for me. With little time left in the game I felt my defense could hold them, but a punt from the end zone was a high-risk play. They had the momentum and they had nothing to lose by sending everyone. With that in mind I chose to run the quarterback out of the back of the end zone on fourth down. That would give us a lot more room for a kick and no rush. The underlining reason was not as obvious but it had a much bigger psychological effect on the other team. It changed them from being confident and aggressive to confused, dossal. Yes I gave them two points but I got the win. Seems they were thinking they had a safety or at least good field position but instead of them getting the safety by great defense and a big boost, I chose to, give it to them and I got at least twenty more yards for them to work from and I got to kick it with my kick off team instead of the punt team. There you go, the safety for offense. Don't be afraid to use it when you need to turn a game around. The psychological aspects are as good or better than the physical ones.

How to slow down a defense

How do you slow down a defense? Let me give you my idea and see if that will work for you. Remember it not so much the play as it is the concept.

If they have eight men in the box and for those of you that may not know what that means it's just the number of defensive players you have within say three to five yards of the line of scrimmage and the ball. So with eight men in the box and they are coming hard on every play and trying to disrupt the play before it really gets going, you need a few plays that will take advantage of this defense. One is the slant pattern, the only defensive players that can stop this play are the linebackers and if they are blitzing, they are going to take themselves out of the play. In addition if you catch them with no safety, you can run this play all the way to the goal line.

Some others you may want to consider are just play action passes. You want them to come hard on the fake run, and then throw the ball over their heads to a tight end or receiver on a short pass pattern, and I want to emphasize short pattern. If they have most of their eight players inside the tackles and a weak end or at least ends that are coming hard to the inside on the play action, then you can try the quick pitch. (Be sure to see the DVD on the quick pitch, running it right is as important as when.) The main thing you are trying to do here is have them start thinking about something other than rushing hard to the backfield. If you can get some yards on these plays they will have to start backing up their linebackers and defensive backs. That will slow the rush and open up the run. The main objective here is to create some room by making the defense backup and spread out thus causing them to hesitate before they make their first move.

Two-minute offense

The two-minute offense is just what it says it is. You have about two minutes to run your offense and get a score. Sometimes I just have to cry when I see big colleges and big pro teams misuse the clock. I run the two-minute drill almost every offensive practice and sometimes on special teams days. The main idea is to get the clock to stop as often as possible. Here are some of the tools you have to get this done:

1. **Time outs**
2. **The sidelines**
3. **Incomplete passes**
4. **In high school and college you have first downs**

Now you see what we have to work with, let's make some plays that take advantage of these tools. Some of the plays we already have - pass plays, plays that move towards the sidelines like sweeps, quick pitch and quarterback keepers. You can also call two plays at the same time, but always run the second one as a sideline or pass play going towards the sideline. The twenty-four and pass twenty-four or twenty-four quarterback keeper would work here. After the first play make sure you get back on the ball as quickly as you can, you don't need a huddle because you already know what play it is. The second play is to the outside and should always be towards the sidelines also making sure you get out-of-bounds to stop the clock. This goes for any play if your player is close to the side-line then make sure you stress the importance of getting out-of-bounds. Remember, hurry up, you have to give them a feeling like this is now or never and it usually is.

The other thing to remember is that if you have things under control and you see you have enough time to get the job done you may want to use more of the clock to insure that they don't have enough time to come back and do the same thing to you. What I do is use plays that set up other plays that I will use when we are ready to score. However if you see the chance to score then you have to weigh the risk of using more time and taking the chance of not getting the score, over taking the score now and leaving time on the clock.

To practice this I will have a coach on a stopwatch and he will count out loud the time as it is ticking down. Later he will only give the time remaining in-between plays. I want them to get a sense of time running out and the feeling to hurry up, which I yell a lot during this drill.

I run the drill and as we go along I point out the mistakes like not getting out of bounds or not running back to the huddle between plays or what-ever the case may be. I will use little or no defense for this drill but I will blow the whistle after I see them get a few yards. Then I always end up on the goal line with little or no time on the clock and one play to win the game. You want that image in their heads that the game was just won by running the right plays and using the clock effectively and the last thing I want them to remember is the win.

Prevent defense
The purpose of this defense is to prevent the score in the last few minutes of a game or the half. The tools for this are the same as the two-minute drill just in reverse:

1. **Make them use their timeouts**
2. **Keep them inbounds**
3. **Keep the clock running**

The approach on this defense is to keep everything in front of you. A first down will not win the game but a long pass for a touchdown will. I don't like to run man coverage any time but for sure not now. With man coverage they only have to beat one defensive back, with zone they have to beat seven defensive backs.

If you have a third and ten you don't need eight guys inside the box. I leave my two down linemen and the ends in to watch the run and to put just enough pressure on the quarterback so he doesn't have too much time to set up and throw the ball. Then I put the linebackers about half way between the line of scrimmage and the first down markers. The defensive backs are about ten to fifteen yards behind them. The safety is back another ten or more behind the defensive backs. If it is a pass play they will drop back into deep pass coverage and if it is a run then the linebackers will come up and the defensive backs will fill in after the ball crosses the line of scrimmage. I'm not too concerned about the first downs as much, but I do not want anybody getting behind my defensive backs.

This is a general set of rules; each game may require a little different line up and adjustments. It will also depend on how big of a lead you have on the other team and what the down and distance is of the next play and not to be left out the time remaining on the clock. If you have a lead with two seconds on the clock and thirty yards for them to get a score you really don't need a lot of people on the line of scrimmage. I would put seven defensive backs in the end zone, four in front and three in the back. Then rush just the two linemen and the two defensives ends. This will put pressure on the quarterback so he doesn't have a lot of time to just sit there and wait for one of his receivers to break lose. After awhile the zone will break down and there will be holes so you don't want to just send two guys in on the rush.

Each game will determine how you run your two minute offense and your prevent defense so be flexible and be smart don't try to out smart yourself and do something dumb. The important thing is to have them in your toolbox sharp and ready to use. I have won many games in the last two minutes that would not have been victories if we didn't have our prevent defense ready to go. This will also hold true with your special plays like the tight end scrape and tight end delay as well as many more. Have them ready but keep them in the toolbox, don't use them until you need them. You will thank me later.

Chapter Nine
First Game

Being ready for the first game is something I have always put a lot of emphasis on; it can set up your whole season. A loss here will put you back a few steps and make it hard to recover. A win here will help propel your team forward and give them a real belief in your program. Something I just realized while writing this book is that as a head coach I never lost an opening game.

Getting excited about the first game is not hard, being ready however is. It started with the first practice. Everything you did was to get you here, so let's back up a bit and make sure you did everything you could to get your team ready. You started on a positive note setting goals and building a belief in you and your program, giving them a feeling of success. You and your coaches were always uplifting and never put anybody down, praising every player on every opportunity. Using every moment to teach good football, good basic techniques and sportsmanship.

Now that you have done all you can to get your team ready for the first game, one thing that I have found to be helpful is to find a team to have a practice game with. Sometimes it will be a team in your own area, someone you don't play during the regular season or maybe if you have a large team you can divide them up and have an inter-squad game amongst your own team. I don't like to have a practice game on the last week before the first game because I want them to be hungry for some hitting. I will build up the hitting to the week just before the first game with some real intense drills like one-on-one, two, three, four and five-on-one tackling (See DVD). But now in the last week I start to back off the hitting and let everything we taught sink in.

Now that we are here and at the last week before a game you have just a few practices before you go out and test your skills with another team. This is the week you want to make any last minute adjustments to your program, nothing too big, little changes maybe. You do your warm-ups the same as always but the drills will be toned down each day till they are more of a discussion and a walk through rather than intense hitting drills. The team drills are the same, slowing down the hitting each day till we are methodically going over each player's assignments.

On the offensive days we will go over each play making sure they are where they should be and every player knows his responsibility. Defensive days are the same, slowing down without any real hitting, just form tackling and on the last day of practice it is a full on walk through, sometimes without any uniforms just a helmet. I make sure we can get on and off the field with all our teams. If you have your own field you can put everybody on one sideline and run them on and off just like you will in a game. In little league you have to hunt for some open grass to simulate a field.

I will run each team on the field and have them run a play or two, then have them come off and run the next team on and have them go through a few plays and continue until all the teams have had a chance to get on and off the field. After the coaching staff is satisfied we end with the two-minute drill and a sit down to give them a little pep talk. We send them home early and tell them to get to bed on time and be to the game with plenty of time to get ready.

In case you didn't catch the point of the last week and day of practice it was shifted to less physical and more physiological. If you haven't taught them well enough in the past month of practice you are not going to do it in the last few days. This last week is to let them absorb all they have been taught and process it all in their heads. This is very important and will prove to be a big help to you in getting ready for the first game.

There was a study done along time ago I'm sorry I can't remember who did it but the point was they took a basketball team and divided them into three groups. They tested them all on the free throw line with a best out of ten free throws. The first team was then sent home for a week and was to report back after that time and be retested. The second team was told to return each day and sit in the stands and visualize the ball going thru the basket and not to touch a ball for the same week. The third group was told to return each day and practice free throws for one hour the same amount of time as the ones who only visualized the free throw. After one week they came back and all were retested. To no ones surprise the team that just went home had no change. The team that practiced every day lost a little and made fewer baskets. To everyone's surprise the team that sat on the bench and visualized the free throws did significantly better. I did the same test on a much smaller scale for myself just to see if it worked on younger kids. I had a Cub Scout group I think around nine year olds or so. I made two groups and tested them all together having them throw ten blocks into a bucket that was about ten feet away. I kept score then sent one set of boys to practice throwing the blocks in the bucket and the other group to sit in a different room and just imagine the blocks going into the bucket. After about ten minutes I brought them all back together and tested them again and just like the basketball test the ones that visualized the blocks going into the bucket did much better than the ones that physically practiced it. I don't want you to think that not practicing will work; I want to say that you also have to leave room for the physiological aspect of the game; you can only do so much physical you have to believe as well. Backing off the physical side of football just before the first game will help them and you internalize and focus on what you all need to do. That is what I try to do before a game as far as giving them some time to think without distractions. I try to keep everything low key until the game starts. Then I will build on every little good thing that happens, I try to brush off the bad and move back to the positive as quickly as I can.

Backing off at practice the week before will help them when they show up at the game, they will have had time to think of their position and all they have to do and they will be ready to hit somebody, in fact they can't wait. Again I try to keep everything low key. I try to have them focus on the mental aspects of the game up until they go out for the opening kick-off. Then I turn them loose and I don't have to do much more than that. They can't help themselves, they will hit anything that gets near them. After that initial outburst I will still try to keep it under control and wait for something good to happen then I jump on that with everything I've got.

I don't want them to be too high before it starts because it is too easy to fall when something bad happens. I like to build on the good and brush off the bad. Don't dwell on the negative; it will only bring more of the same. Focus on the positive keep their minds busy on the good and what we are going to do next. This will help to keep them thinking on what we can do instead of what we can't.

Now when we get to the game I always want to be on offense first. I will always choose to receive the ball first because I want to score first and I think I can, that will set the tone for the defense. On defense I will blitz a lot at first because I think the other team will start slowly and with simple plays just like me. This will usually work and we get the ball back after they go three and out. I will try hard to score again and if I do that will pretty much put me in control of the rest of the game and let me just stay with my first level plays. If not I will work real hard to score and get the lead pulling out every play I need to do that. Except my very, very special plays. I want to save what I can incase it comes down to the last seconds of the game. As long as I am in the lead I will save most of my big plays, but believe me I am not afraid to pull them out in a pinch.

After the first game you will see if you made all the right decisions on where everybody should be. For the most part that will hold true with me but I have made some changes after the first game to improve the team a little. I usually don't change very much.

After each game I will always reflect back on it and see where we can improve, there is always something you can do better. I will have to say that I will reflect more after a loss than a win.

The practices will get a little different after the first game, more like a classroom and more specific to the next team you will be playing. If you can scout the next team you will be playing you will adjust your practice to what that team does on offense and defense to help you get ready for them. If you can draw up some of the other teams plays on an 8 1/2 by 11 inch cardstock and use them to run your scout team. You can do this for offense as well as defense. I hold up the card and have the scout team see it and run it to the best of their ability. The scout team is a very important part of the program, if you saw the movie Rudy you remember the part where the first string linemen tells him to back down and not try so hard,

Rudy replies back, "My job is to make you a better player so no I won't back down." Remember the scout team is very important and should be looked at and treated that way.

In little league you will not have the luxury of a scout team but I will use what players I have as the scout team and rotate them in and out of the first team to give everybody a chance to play on both sides. There will be times when you will have the first team in for a long time so go over some important plays, but don't forget the rest of the team - everybody is important.

I will save plays but I never tell or let the team know that is what we are doing. I use whatever play I need to win but I never hold back, I don't want my team to think that any team is not worth a complete effort every time. That is when you lose because you thought they were not as good as you.

Now that we have all the tools ready we want to get into the real game of football, the game that we all love and think is the only one on the planet. In the next chapter we will look at the what, where and how this is all supposed to work and try to put it into perspective as if we are in a game like situation.

Chapter Ten
How to Play Football

Let's start from the beginning and go all the way thru to a game like situation and I will try to give you a feel of the how, why and when of football. There is a way to use everything you've seen in this book, to take advantage of the other teams good and bad or strengths and weaknesses, but first let me say that I don't care what offense or defense you want to run, I have seen them all work and all fail. It's not what you run but how you run it. I will use what I run mostly to demonstrate what I am talking about, this will give you a starting point but remember what works for me may not work for you.

What I use is a basic slot right with an "I" formation. Occasional I will split the backs for certain plays but to start with I always use an "I" backfield unless I say split in the call. I like to think I use a balanced combination of run and pass but I will pass more if that is what the other team gives me or I will run more if that is what's there.

On defense I run a split six with a lot of blitzes but only when the situation calls for it, either way I want you to try and not focus on the type of offense or defense but the concepts and take the big picture approach. Then try to discover what will work for you, take that and work on developing your own program that best suits your style.

Offense

A lot of coaches like to start off with the one they ran in high school or college, mainly because that is the one they know the best. You may want to start there then let yourself move to what works for you and what will work for the teams you will be coming up against during the year. As you start to build your program you may have a great play you ran as a kid or maybe you saw on TV or while watching another game somewhere. Try to remember that the play works for a reason, either it was run at the right time or in the right place or it was set up by a play or two that was run before it, and for sure it was executed properly. Look for the details that make that play great. Another thing to remember is you can take most plays you see on TV or whatever and make them your own and alter them to fit your program.

When I was an assistant coach on a high school team I took a few of my plays and adapted them to the veer that was being run by that head coach. Let me show you a couple of these plays to give you an example of how it can be done. Take a look at them and hopefully you can get an idea on how adapting a play might work for you. First the basic veer, then the adapted version of the tight end delay and the twenty-three cross.

Basic veer

Pass twenty-two tight end delay

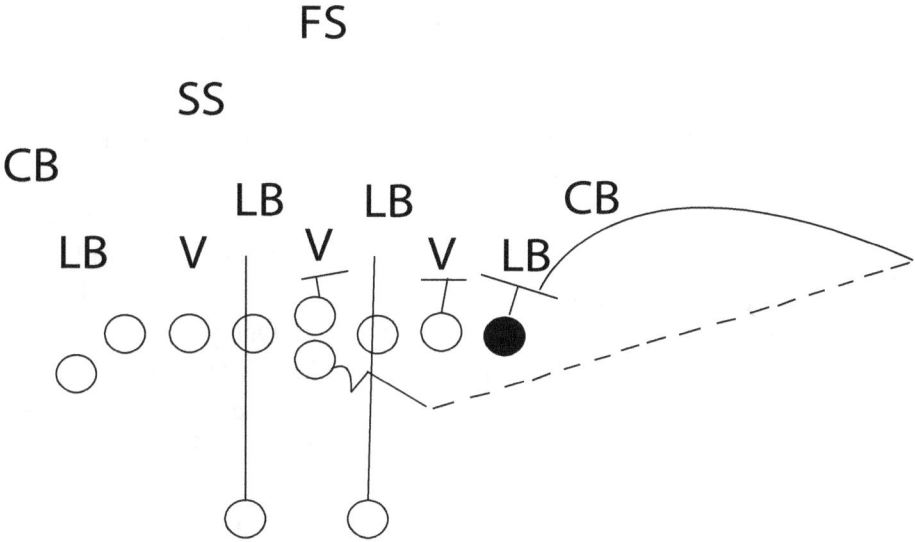

Twenty-three cross

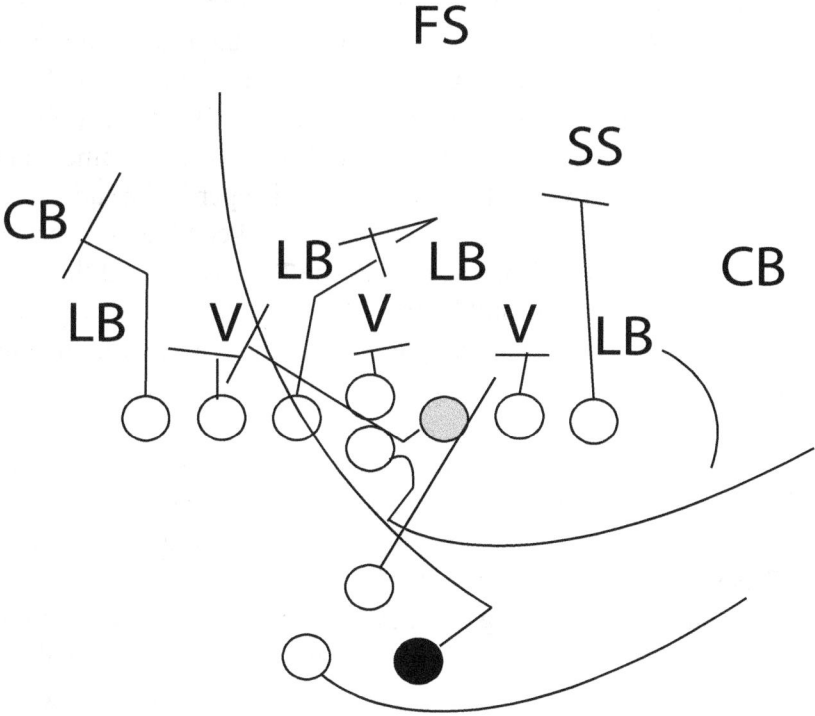

You can start with virtually any play and find a way to make it work for you in a host of different applications. These are only a couple to get you started, draw up your best play and then work something off of it and keep building until you have what you want and need.

I feel there are certain plays like these two I adapted for the veer that you must have in your program, think of them as tools in your toolbox, if you don't have the right tool it makes the job a lot harder. I know you all have tried to pound something in with a pair of pliers and thought if I only had a hammer. The right tool for the job can make the task a lot easer. Let's go back a bit and start with the basic concept first. One you have to have a great something, let's use a boxer as an example. Think of it as a big jab to the gut, it knocks the wind out of you and you have to take a second to catch your breath. The boxer keeps throwing that punch till you lower your hands even if it's just a little. Now when you see that punch coming you brace for it and lower your hands even farther. But to your surprise you get hit with a right cross to the face instead. Your instinct tells you to bring your hand back up, so you follow your tendency and move your hands up, just in time to take another to the gut. Football is the same thing; I use a twenty-four and a few more plays to the right of my offense as my jab to the gut. I do that until they adjust to it by moving defensive players to my right side. Then I work some plays off the twenty-four as a right cross. For example, pass twenty-four. It starts off the same and then ends up different. The twenty-four quarterback keeper is the same as the twenty-four, the difference is the quarterback will keep it and go around the end, it looks the same from the defense point of view until they see the quarterback running outside and by then they are chasing the play. You want to do the same with whatever play you want to start with, then build off of that.

These two plays put a lot of pressure on the defense, they are never quite sure if you are running, passing or is the quarterback keeping it. You will find out quickly if they are able to defend the run and the pass at the same time. These two plays are just the start. What I do from here will depend on what the other team is doing and how they are adjusting to my plays, that will tell me what I want to do next. As you saw in the play calling section I try to make the play calling as simple as I can. Twenty-four, pass twenty-four and twenty-four quarterback keeper are basically the same plays to the linemen, backs and receivers and it looks the same to the defense at first, the difference is the end result. Twenty-four the two back gets the ball. Pass twenty-four one of the receivers gets the ball or the quarterback will keep it (depending on if and who's open). Twenty-four quarterback keeper, the quarterback keeps it much like a sweep, but let's go back to the jab or whatever play is your power play or like a lot of people like to call it, your bread and butter play. This jab and right cross combination will work for you on many plays and in many situations. Remembering that it's not so much the play as it is the concept. I am going to try to show this in another set of plays I like to call the hand is quicker than the eye.

I run plays to my right side like the twenty-four and others that start like it. I do that for a while or until they start leaning to my right side by putting more players over there or slant the defense to that side. When I say slanting to that side I mean they will have the linemen go to my right side as their first move after the ball is snapped. When I see that I will go back to the other side or my left with a few plays like the twenty-three cross. This play starts out like a twenty-four but the two back cuts back to the three hole.

If you are running the twenty-four well and then you see they adjust to it and start to slow it down or stop it you need to run the twenty-three cross

As they see the twenty-four start these three guys will take off to the right to stop the runner and take themselves out of the play

After the back clears the line there will only be two guys left the safety and the corner back

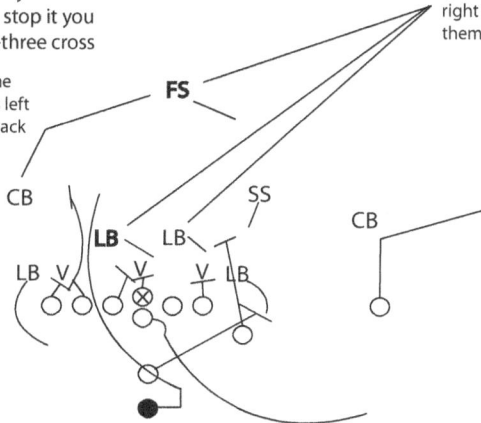

FS

CB   SS

LB   LB

LB   LB

CB

This play will always get a lot of yards and makes the opposing coaches start second guessing themselves and making them have to decide whether they will stay on my right or keep people on the left side, my left. Then I run a thirty-three dive to help them with that decision. I want them to keep people on my left, then I go back to the right. I don't care if the thirty-three goes for a fifty yard touchdown or not, as long as it gains some yards. I am running that play to set up another play. Without fail the coach on the other side will tell his outside linebacker and defensive back, "When you see that play get up in there." As soon as you see the outside linebacker move up close to the line of scrimmage you are ready to throw the right cross, which is the twenty-nine quick pitch or the pass thirty-three tight end delay. However setting this play up is only half the battle, running it correctly is the other half.

The defense will take a step to the
right towards the fake thirty-two
that will give the two back a head start

FS

CB   SS   CB
        LB   LB
LB V   V   V   LB

2   3

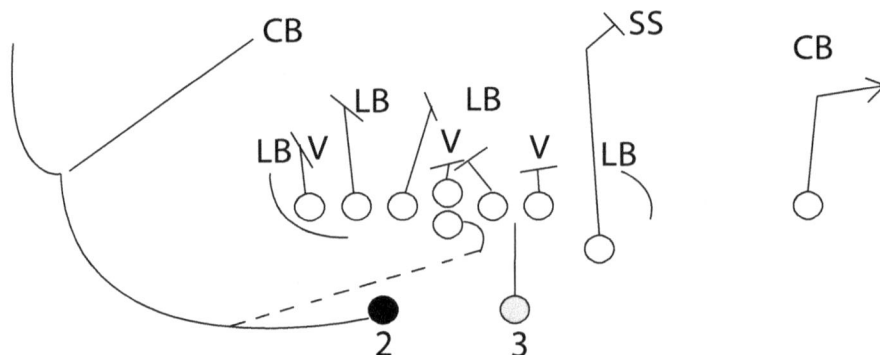

I will try to save the pass thirty-three tight end delay if I can. If you don't remember the keys to this play go back and review them, they are very important and will have to be understood to make this play work. One very important detail is that the tight end makes a block on the outside linebacker or tight end, then releases into the pass pattern which can be a number of different patterns. Urban Myer from Florida uses a variation of this play from the shot-gun but he has the quarterback who moves towards the line of scrimmage to fake a dive play. He puts his head down which I feel is a very important detail to this play for him. Then the quarterback does a jump pass to the tight end. The pattern he runs is usually a little streak to the back of the end zone. He will save this play mostly for the goal line; I haven't seen him use it in the middle of the field myself but I can't watch every game he plays, however I have used my version on short yardage when I really need a big play.

The corner back will come up on the fake

FS

CB

SS

CB

LB

LB

LB

V

V

LB

LB

Right

Left   Left

The tight end must make a block on the outside linebacker or D-end then releases into the pass pattern

QB foot work

A side note to remember is that this play will not work on long yardage downs because the linebackers are too far back. When and where you use this play is as important as the play. For me the tight end will run a very short sideline pattern, if he goes too deep he will pick up the defensive back or safety and we don't want that.

Having a great play is only great when you know how to use it or where. In addition the details of the play are equally as important. This play as well as a few more I will show you must be kept under lock and key till you need them. Never show more than you need to win the game. Not to say I keep all my plays a secret I don't. I can give my playbook to the other team before a game and they still wouldn't know what to do with it. They don't know when, where or even if I'm going to run a particular play. I don't even know for sure myself if I will run a particular play until I see something on the field that makes me think of it. So when I say under lock and key I mean more like in the toolbox. I save that tool for when the situation calls for it. I'm not going to run the tight end delay just for fun. When the game is on the line, I may need it to convert a third and short or a third and goal. Keep it in the box till it is the right tool for the job.

Another play (tool) I would like go over at this time that I feel is essential to any football contractors toolbox is the spread formation tight end slant.

FS

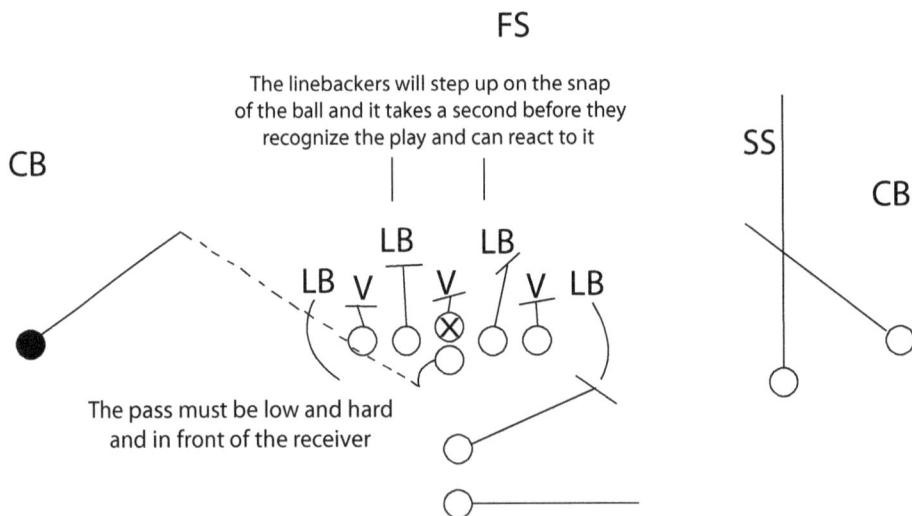

The linebackers will step up on the snap of the ball and it takes a second before they recognize the play and can react to it

CB

SS

CB

LB LB

LB V V V LB

The pass must be low and hard and in front of the receiver

This play is used to get a first down when the yardage is short and the linebackers are up close to the line of scrimmage same as the tight end delay, but you can't always use the tight end delay every time you need a short and goal or third and short. The slant can be used for more situations and the pattern can be adjusted to fit more yardage if needed. The only defensive player that can make the play on this pass pattern is the linebacker, but not if he is close to the line of scrimmage. The keys to this play are very simple, the first two I already said and the others are, first, the pass must be low and hard and most important in front of the receiver. Second, the quarterback must be quick. He has no time to think about setting his feet or read the defense or anything for that matter just get the ball on its way A.S.A.P. I should call this a quick slant because there are a few longer ones but for me I only use the quick slant, so to separate it from the others for me is unnecessary. Third, it must be run from a spread formation or a split out set for the wide receiver. The other points are the backs run to the line or the right and the linemen block low and hard. The linebackers will step up on the snap of the ball and it will take a second for them to recognize the play and react to it. One of the reasons this play works well is the defense will put their best defensive back on the wide receiver and the second best on the slot back, leaving the tight end out wide with their number three defensive back; but after they see this play they will most likely make an adjustment. This is not a play I save to often in fact I want them to know about this play, it is another jab to the gut. I run it a few times then when I see the coach on the other side tell his corner back to move up and to the inside. That is my sign to go for six, that's six points my friend. For this I hit them with a tight end slant pump and go.

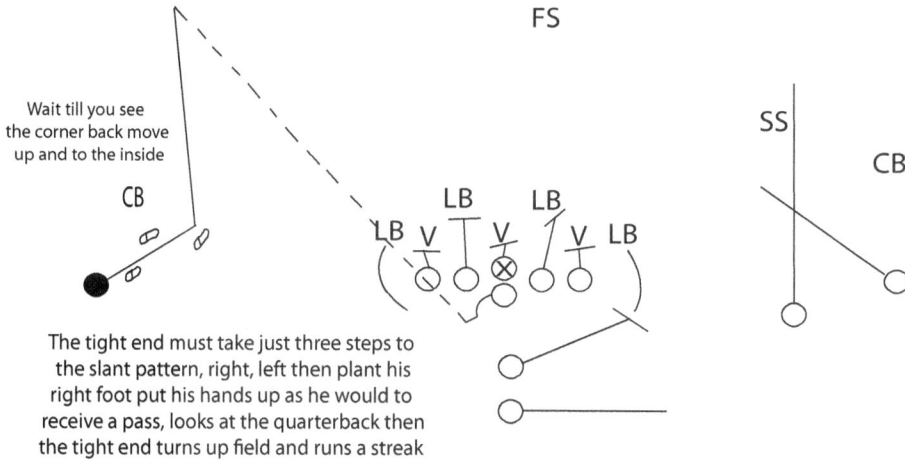

FS

Wait till you see
the corner back move
up and to the inside

SS

CB

CB

LB

LB

LB

V

V

V

LB

CB

The tight end must take just three steps to
the slant pattern, right, left then plant his
right foot put his hands up as he would to
receive a pass, looks at the quarterback then
the tight end turns up field and runs a streak

I only run the spread on a few plays because I want them to think they know the slant is coming. It makes me smile. The keys are this. One, the quarterback again has to be quick and I mean quick, he stands up and makes the fake or the pump then he throws the go pattern. He has to release the ball before the tight end brakes free, but don't worry it's always open, that is if the tight end runs it right. The tight end must take just three steps to the slant pattern, right, left, then plant his right foot put his hands up as he would to receive a pass, looks at the quarterback then turns up field and runs a streak. If the defensive back jumps the route he will take himself out of the play. If your tight end is fast it's six, if not it is at least twenty to thirty yards before the safety or anybody can catch him. You might want to see the DVD on this one because it is faster than you think and until you see it in action it is sometimes hard to get it. The same might be true for the tight end delay. Watch both plays and remember it's the little things I want you to notice, where are his feet and where is the receiver looking?

There are any number of plays this concept will work on. When you have your big play then use it to set up your second level plays and then you can develop the ones you like that will work best for you. Now that you have a jab and right cross you can keep building on them and remember you need more than one. The slant is a right cross and the slant pump and go is another right cross to the first right cross or maybe we can call it a combination like a right cross and uppercut.

Every game will be different so don't think every great play will work in every game, be ready to adjust and invent when you see something you did not expect. Let's take another situation and try to work it.

Let's say you have been running awhile and you see they have moved up their linebackers and defensive backs close to the line of scrimmage and playing to stop your running game. It maybe time to go with a few passes. Look over what they are doing to stop your running game then make your adjustments according to that. Take your big play whatever that may be. For me it's the slot right twenty-four, then build a pass off of it. Pass twenty-four can be run as a running play or a pass play depending on what I need. I can also run more or different passes off of the twenty-four, I can change the call to a slot right pass twenty-four and then add different patterns to it by just adding it to the end of the call like a slot right pass twenty-four slot back quick post, if there is no safety in the middle or if he is deep and over to the right to stop the sprint out pass, then this would be a play you could run to take advantage of that alignment. You can also try a slot right pass twenty-four slot back hook if the safety is in the middle of

Slot right pass 24 slot back quick post

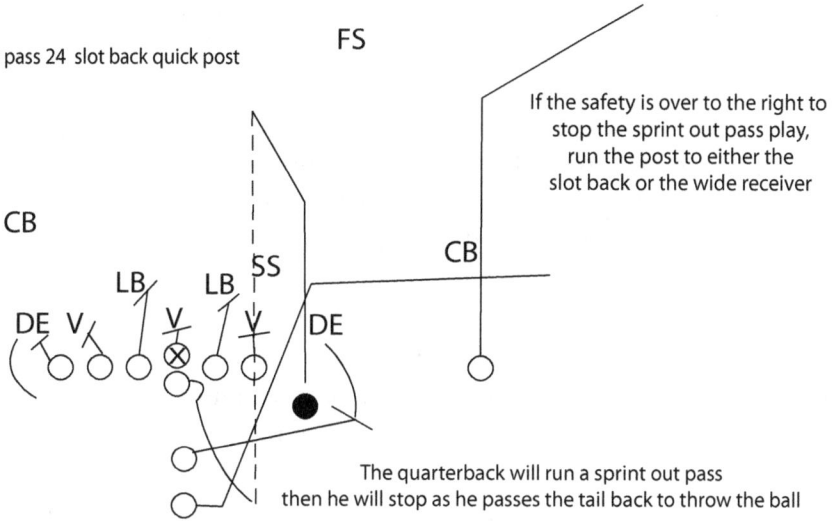

FS

If the safety is over to the right to
stop the sprint out pass play,
run the post to either the
slot back or the wide receiver

CB

CB

LB   LB   SS

DE V   V   V   DE

The quarterback will run a sprint out pass
then he will stop as he passes the tail back to throw the ball

the field and still deep. This will only work if you run it from the twenty-
four or some kind of play action in the backfield, if not the strong safety
or linebackers will get in the way and knock it down or intercept it. If
the safety is over to the right to stop the sprint out pass then run the post
to the slot back. If the safety is coming up on the slot back hook pattern
then you will want to run the post to the wide receiver. On these plays
the backs will start out the same as the twenty-four but on a pass play the

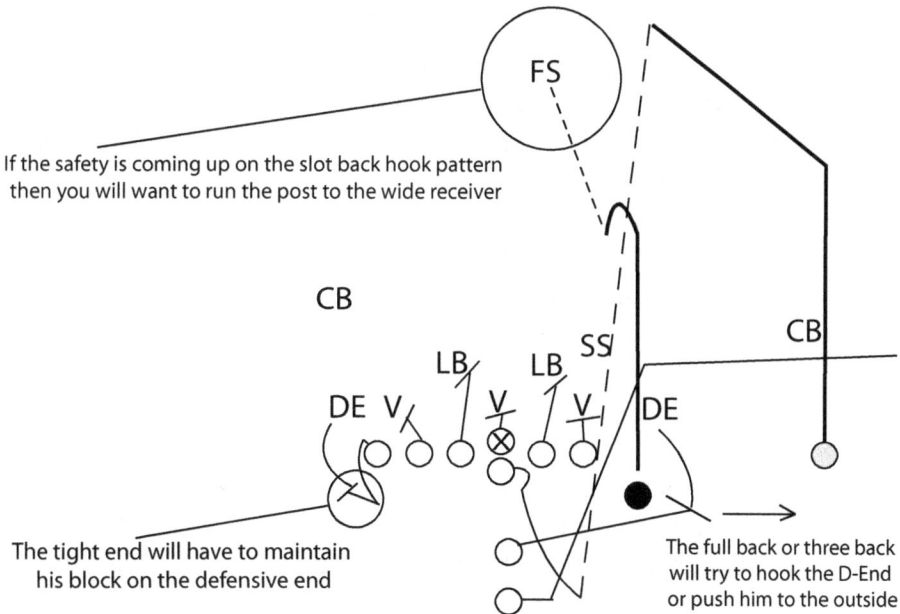

FS

If the safety is coming up on the slot back hook pattern
then you will want to run the post to the wide receiver

CB

CB

LB   LB   SS

DE V   V   V   DE

The tight end will have to maintain
his block on the defensive end

The full back or three back
will try to hook the D-End
or push him to the outside

full back or three back will try to hook the end instead of block him out like on a twenty-four. The tailback or two back will run the same as the twenty-four. He will not get the ball but will try to look like he did, that will bring the linebackers forward this will help clear out the middle for the slot back. The quarterback will run a sprint out pass then he can stop as he passes the tailback to throw the ball if it's a hook pattern. If it's a wide receiver post, then he will go a little further before he throws the ball. This play takes a little better quarterback to execute because he has to be able read the safety and defensive back to decide who to throw the ball to. He will also have to find him in the center of the field quickly before the linemen get to him. Last he must be able to hit the receiver with the pass. A side note to this play is that the tight end has to stay and help on the block because the quarterback is venerable if he is a right handed passer, so the tight end will have to maintain his block on the defensive end to allow the quarterback time to pass.

For me using the sprint out or play action backfield to pass helps to keep the linebackers in tight and makes more room for the pass patterns. It also leaves one-on-one coverage on your receivers most of the time. The thing to remember with these plays and whatever plays you like to run is if you have a great play you need to have five more off of it. Use your big play a lot and make sure everybody knows it and hopefully make them adjust to it, then hit them with the right cross. Build your program with the idea that you will need plays off of the big play and if they stop this play, what can I do off of it to take advantage of that adjustment? Start thinking of your plays as first level, second level, and so on and always have your big down and distance plays that you can bring out of your toolbox when you need them; like my third and very long play - the pass twenty-four tight end scrape. I have gone without using this play in games but I was sure glad it was in my toolbox when I needed it. This is my big yardage on big downs play. This play starts out like a pass twenty-four same as always but this time the wide receiver and the slot back run a post while the tight end runs a five to seven yard scrape pattern. The tight end starts from all the way on the other side of the formation and must stay underneath the defensive backs and behind the linebackers. The key points to this play are, first, the quarterback must get a little deeper than normal but not too deep that he tips off the play, just

158

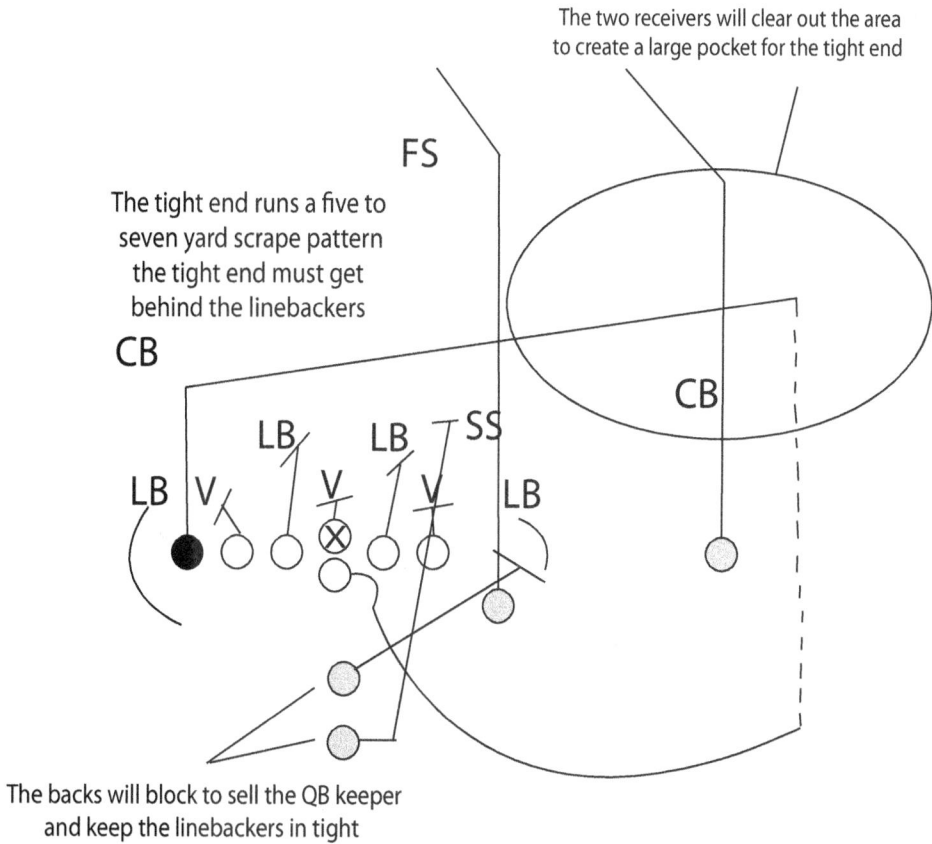

The two receivers will clear out the area to create a large pocket for the tight end

FS

The tight end runs a five to seven yard scrape pattern the tight end must get behind the linebackers

CB

LB   LB   SS

LB   CB

LB   V   V   V   LB

The backs will block to sell the QB keeper and keep the linebackers in tight

enough to give himself some time to set up the play. The two receivers will clear out the area and create a large pocket for the tight end. The tight end has to get behind the linebackers or they will follow him. The quarterback waits till the area clears and then seemingly out of nowhere the tight end comes out of the pack and makes the catch. He will have time to turn up field because the defensive backs are following the two receivers and the linebackers came up to bite on the fake twenty-four then they will go after the quarterback thinking it is a quarterback keeper. That is why you have to run the twenty-four and the keeper before this play will work. The defensive end is chasing the quarterback as well so that leaves a big gap in the pass coverage. It is a nice easy pass, you don't have to throw it hard or fast just as long as it gets there. This play was one I got from BYU back in the eighties, they ran this a lot but of course they ran it from a drop back pass attack and I had to adjust it to a play action approach. This play actually works better for me than it did for them and it worked great for them. This play even worked on a prevent defense but I don't know why.

Now let's say they put eight guys in the box and the safety is back off the line more than ten yards, I will run a slot right pass twenty-four slot back sideline. The corner back goes with the wide receiver and the safety cannot make up the distance when he sees the slot back run the sideline. If they are in a zone the first steps of the safety will be back as well as the corner backs. That leaves the corner back with a decision either he will come up on the sideline pattern of the slot back or take the wide receiver back a ways on his post pattern. The linebackers came up on the fake twenty-four so all the quarterback has to do is read the corner back, if he goes back then the slot back is open, if he comes up then the wide receiver is open and he will have to hit the seam of the zone. Almost all the time it is the slot back who is open because their coach just like me says, "Don't let anybody get behind you." The linebackers will be out of the play because they have stepped up on the twenty-four fake and then come up thinking it's a quarterback keeper. If not, run the twenty-four and the quarterback keeper again.

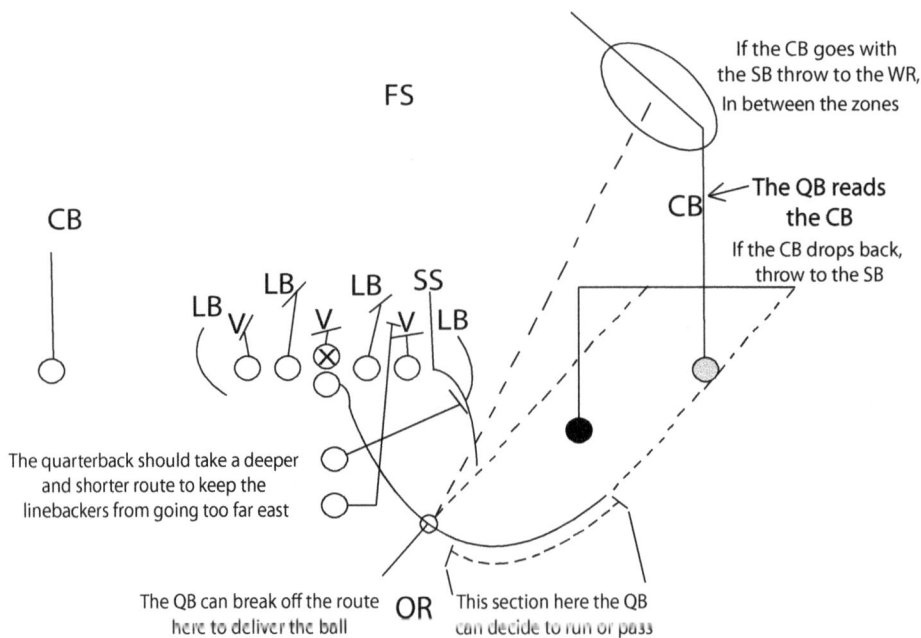

If the CB goes with the SB throw to the WR, In between the zones

FS

The QB reads the CB

If the CB drops back, throw to the SB

CB

CB

LB LB LB SS LB

The quarterback should take a deeper and shorter route to keep the linebackers from going too far east

The QB can break off the route here to deliver the ball OR This section here the QB can decide to run or pass

The play is basically the same with the exception of the pass patterns and they can be adjusted to fit the defense you are running against. You want to design your pass plays off of your running plays or like BYU used to do is design your run plays off your pass plays. It really doesn't matter which comes first, with BYU it was pass first run second with Air Force it is run first pass second both work and work well, it doesn't matter as long as you make sure your big plays are executed perfectly and everybody knows it, then you can build off of that.

You can also design your run plays off of other run plays like my twenty-four and my twenty-three cross. When I was in the early days of being a head coach I saw another hole develop off to the left side when I ran the twenty-four. I thought about it for a while and developed a new play that I called a twenty-three cross. It was a way to take advantage of what I saw. I started running this play from a split backfield but it didn't work so I tried it from an "I" backfield and found that it made a much bigger difference. I wanted the play to look like a twenty-four for as long as possible to make the defense think that is what it was, then I made the adjustment to the three hole with as little change as possible. I wanted it to look like the original play. The same is true with the pass patterns and pass plays, if you have a great pass play see what the defense is doing to defend it then adjust to it with a new pattern like the pass twenty-four tight end scrape. I saw the defense coming hard to the quarterback and the defensive backs going deep with the receivers so I wanted to find a way to take advantage of their aggressiveness. When I saw the play run at BYU I wanted to see if I could design it to fit my program. I just thought about it and came up with my version of the play.

From here we need to go to what I call, game like situations and try to show what I might do in certain situations of the game and for different down and distances.

When I go into a game I always want the ball first that is because I think I can score every time I'm on offense. We know that just isn't true but that's the way I think. So, if we win the toss I want the ball. I also feel that a quick score will set the tone for the game and give me the edge. If I get the ball I will run a return right and save the miss direction in case they score. My first play is the slot right twenty-four I want to see how they set up for it and how well they scouted me. If we made yards on the twenty-four you can bet I'm going to run it again and again till they stop it. I will however mix it up with a few pass twenty-fours and twenty-four quarter-back keepers. Again if I'm making yards to the right I will stay with it till they stop me. When I first run pass twenty-four I will tell the quarterback that I want him to run first even if someone is open, if they come after him then pass it. I want to see how they defend it. Now I want to run the thirty-three to get a look at the left side defensive backs and linebackers. I will always have someone looking at the defensive end on the left side to see when we can run the reverse but I want to tell right away where the defensive backs are and what they are doing.

After that I will run what works or to what I think is their weakness but like I just said If they can't stop the right side I will just keep running there until they stop me or the game ends. If they are coming hard to the twenty-four and slowing it down or stopping it I will run a twenty-three cross. Now that we tighten up the left side and move the defensive back a little closer to the line of scrimmage I want to take advantage of that with a tight end slant. Now I feel like I have them guessing on defense and thinking too much. I want them to move the defensive backs and line-backers off the line of scrimmage. I want to take advantage of the defense and get a few yards. Hopefully that will move me into scoring position and help me set up the plays I want to use to score. I know what plays I want to use for this so let's set it up. When I'm in position to score I want to run the middle and to the right first and then run the plays that go with the ones I ran to get here. Example, if I ran to the right most of the time and used the twenty-four and the twenty-three cross I will go with a quarterback bootleg to score. If I ran the slant and the thirty-three or to the left side I will go with a pass thirty-three tight end delay as my scoring play, if I didn't have to use the pass twenty-four to get down here I will go with that one and tell the quarterback to get the score. I don't care if he runs it in or has to pass it "just do it."

In general if I am trying to back up the linebackers to give us a little more room to run the ball inside I will run to the outside with a quick pitch or more quarterback keepers. If I can't get outside I will go to a more serious passing attack, starting with a pass twenty-four and then maybe back to a tight end or wide receiver slant. Maybe if I need to I will adjust the patterns on the pass twenty-four. Let me explain this to give you an idea of some of the ways you can make a few adjustments to your pass plays to give you more options.

One is if they are eight in the box with the free safety in the middle of the field and the strong safety on the line as one of the eight I will go with a spread right twenty-four wide receiver post slot back sideline; remember the last part of the call is where I want the ball to go. (This play is back a few pages if you want to take another look at it.) This slot back sideline pattern will take advantage of the safety being so far back and give him a chance to decide if he want to move up and guard the slot back or stay back and help with the deep coverage, because his coach just like me always says, "Don't let anybody get behind you." The defensive back will almost always take the wide receiver and go deep because he was told the same thing, "Don't let anybody behind you."

If they move the safety up on the slot back I go with a wide receiver post because now there is no free safety to help with the long ball. If they move the strong safety over to guard the slot back I will go back to the run. (Side note if you run this slot back sideline from the spread you will have to move the slot back in a little to allow room to the outside for the sideline pattern.) If you ran the tight end slant previously the free safety will stay in the middle of the field, and again if not then you can go back to the tight end slant or the tight end slant pump and go and pick up six points.

If they leave the safety in the middle of the field and the strong safety goes to cover the slot back then a great play to use is the wide receiver post flag. This play and pass route is not on the pass route hand out I gave in the first of the book because I wanted to keep it as simple as I could, but this is just an example of what you can do or think up when you need to. The basic play is already there so all you are doing is adding a little different pass route.

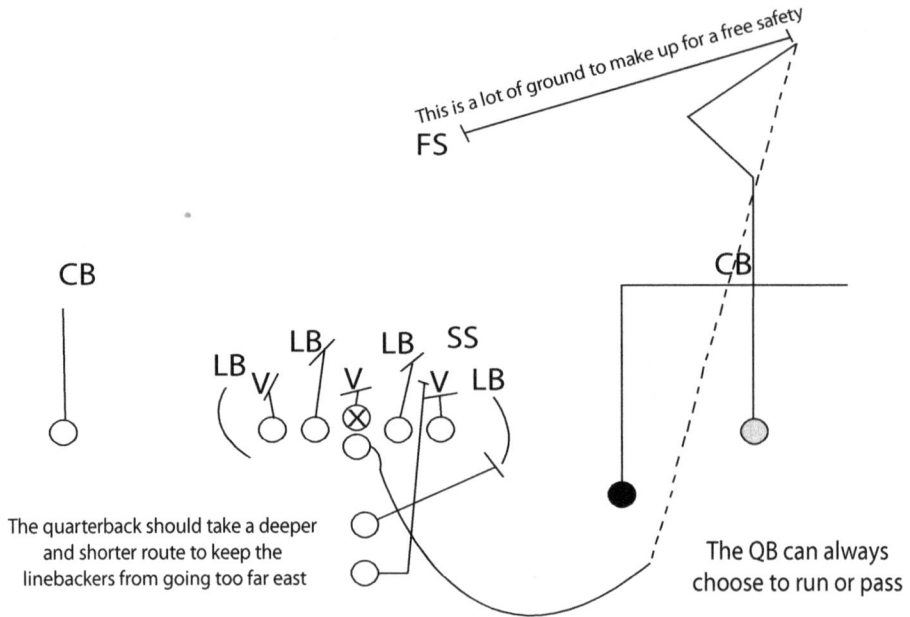

This is a lot of ground to make up for a free safety

FS

CB

CB

LB LB SS

LB V V V LB

The quarterback should take a deeper and shorter route to keep the linebackers from going too far east

The QB can always choose to run or pass

A post flag is a great play if you want to get a quick score or get them to back up or pull the strong safety off the line of scrimmage and back into coverage where he belongs. The wide receiver goes on a post route then after he passes the corner back, he makes a right turn to the flag. The safety has to make up a lot of ground in a short period of time and seldom can achieve this lofty goal. If you run these plays successfully they will have to back the strong safety up to cover the deep half of the field. If they do that then go back to the run, if not keep passing the ball.

Let's go to the goal line again and take another look at a few more things that might be important in deciding what to do in certain situations pertaining to the goal line. As you get in close to the goal line things get a little tight and that is why you see a lot of teams go all the way down to the red zone and then lose it all when they get in close. I hear a lot of coaches and insightful announcers say, "They got down here with the pass why don't they stay with it?" Well, that is because they didn't set up the pass well enough before they got down to the red zone or they didn't set up the run first, either way you have to think ahead before you get there and have your plays ready to go when you do. Example, I just saw a game on TV where the quarterback ran the ball five times in a row to get down to the two-yard line with a first and goal. On the next play they ran the quarterback again and he was dropped for a loss so they ran the quarter-back again but was dropped for another loss. Now it was third and goal from the seven-yard line. I was perplexed to see them run the quarterback again. I scratched my head and said take the field goal and take the lead, but to my dismay they ran the quarterback again on a draw and this time he slipped and fell on the five and they came away with no points. For your consideration please think of this sequence of plays. First and goal on the two, I run a twenty-four, not caring if they stop it or not. Then I will try a thirty-three again not caring that much if it gets the score or not, I am more interested in the next play that will only work if I ran the other two first. Now that I have them in nice and close thinking run inside, I have the choice of either a pass twenty-four quarterback keeper or a thirty-three tight end delay or what I think will work well in this situation is the slot right twenty-four quarterback bootleg. I like this one because I also was watching the defensive end on the left side to see if he takes a hard line to the inside to try to stop the run and if the linebacker comes up on the play to the line of scrimmage. When you are this close to the goal line they have to respect the inside running play and that is why the play action and the miss direction plays are so important in this part of the field. But before the play action will work you have to set it up. If they don't respect the run play down here, then you would have scored already with the twenty-four or the thirty-three. It is basic physics, it reminds me of the old saying about money and interest, "Those that understand interest receive it and those that don't pay it." "Those that understand physics score, those that don't get scored upon." I just made that up but it sounds right doesn't it? We will explore that concept a little later because I think that basic physics are a major part of football, but I will have to think on that for a while and draw up some diagrams to support what's going on in my head. For the time being let's get back to the third and goal on the two. In case you missed it I started with plays that hit hard to the middle and went forward towards the goal line and not back. I see a lot of teams get down to the goal line and then start there way backwards and turn a first and goal on the two into a third and goal on the ten. Not only do you want to get closer each time but set up the next play or the big right cross for third and goal or fourth and goal if that is what is needed.

I know before the season starts what I want to run inside the ten and for a third and short. I design the play or plays for that very purpose so that when I am in that situation I have the play or plays ready to go. I also have the situations set up because I set it up in the plays I ran prior to getting down to the goal line. You can't run the quarterback six times in a row and expect them to think pass on third and goal. If you want to run the quarterback six times in a row that's ok, then when you get in scoring territory you fake the quarterback keeper and toss it over their heads to someone that was not involved in the plays previous to getting down to the goal line. Set it up before you get in scoring territory so that when you are there you are ready with your big plays or your right cross. I set up the bootleg with the two runs to the inside, now I have the quarterback fake the hand off to the two back on the fake twenty-four, then roll slowly with his back to the defense for a second to the left side, then run like crazy to the corner of the end zone. If he didn't make it still I have yet another play standing by in the form of the bootleg tight end wiggle.

The thing you don't want to do is go backwards when you are in this close, spending as little time in the backfield as possibly, reducing the chances of losing yards. Do the math if you have a first and goal from the five then you have three to make five that is a little over 1.6 yards per play and less if you want to count fourth down. You can almost fall down that much but not if you start off going sideways and six yards back in the backfield. Hit the hole fast and hard and save the level two plays till you need them.

Little league notes
In little league the games are about one hour to an hour and a half long so you don't have a lot of time to set things up. It is imperative that you start early and use the clock to your advantage. I put a lot more energy into first downs as well as touchdowns. Sure I will score when I see the opportunity but I want to use the clock as much as I can in the process. I have been in games where I scored twice in the first quarter and the other team only had the ball for three plays and a kick, that's three and out. They didn't have the time to set things up and I took advantage of that. I want first downs first and I want scores at the end, that is my goal and that's what works for me. I want to get off of defense as soon as I can, that will give me a better chance to score and reduce theirs.

It's all about risk management and percentages. What is the highest percentage of success for the plays you want to run whether it is on offense or defense? It doesn't matter as long as you can manage the risk and use the highest level of success to get you where you want to be. If you have a great defense you can be a little more aggressive on offense, if you can score easy then you can take more of a risk on defense. However all of this information may not be available to you till after the game starts and you can assess the situation and decide where you can take the risks and where to be conservative. It's never the same but having the plays ready is the first step on offense and defense. In high school and above you will have time to set up your plays and you can be patient. In the younger ages you have to be quick and think on your feet. You rarely get a chance to scout the other team because they will play at the same time as you and on the other side of town. You can't send your assistant coaches, you need them to help you in your game so that leaves the parents and they won't go, they want to watch little Johnny play on your team. So then as you can see you will have to be ready for anything and be flexible and ready to adjust.

Defense

The split six defense is basically eight guys in the box set up to stop the run, that is the first thing I want to do and that is my defensive strategy. In the younger ages they will run more than pass so if you can stop the run then they have to adjust and try something different. If you are lucky they will have to go to a less familiar attack which will give you the edge.

I try to stop the run first and if I am successful and I get them into a passing mode I will start to play a regular read defense and not blitz so much. I don't like to blitz when I think it's going to be a pass I would rather defend it with a zone and try to keep everything in front of me and "Let no man get behind my secondary for a big play."

Playing defense is just as much a mind game as offense. I try to force them into what I want and then shut that down. I can use the split six defense to blitz from any angle to help them decide what I want. Once I have them thinking too much I have a better chance to take over the game. I love defense but I only love it for three downs and a kick.

I start with blitzes to try to disrupt their plays before they get any confidence and before they try to set me up. With that in mind I will start with the inside linebackers and send them on some blitzes. The first one is always a right side outside left side inside that puts both linebackers going to the left, that is because most teams run to the left most of the time (our left - their right).

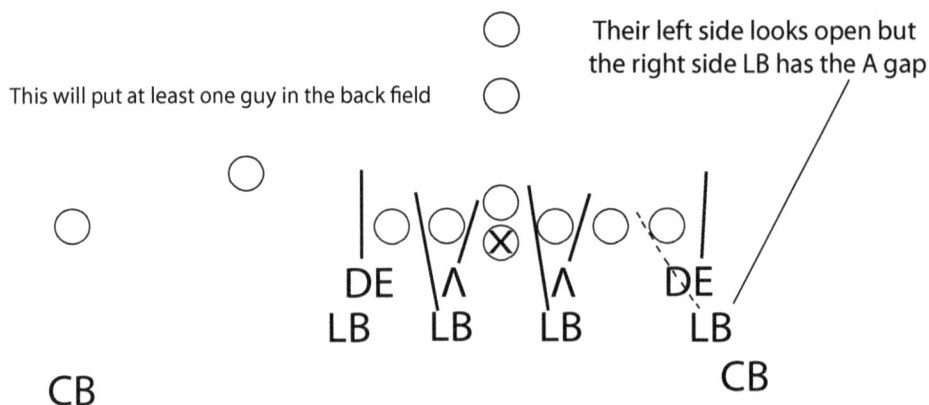

Their left side looks open but the right side LB has the A gap

This will put at least one guy in the back field

DE   DE
LB   LB   LB   LB
CB   CB

FS   As the D-backs drop back in coverage they will keep an eye on the receiver closest to them

I will blitz at first because I think they are going to be conservative to start and I can get my guys in their backfield to disrupt the play and help them to not get any confidence. If they are a good team and they get a first down I will pull back the blitzing for a time so they don't get used to it. As they approach the red zone I will start up with the blitzes again. I will send the inside linebackers most of the time and let the defensive ends and outside linebackers play regular. Then I will send the outside line-

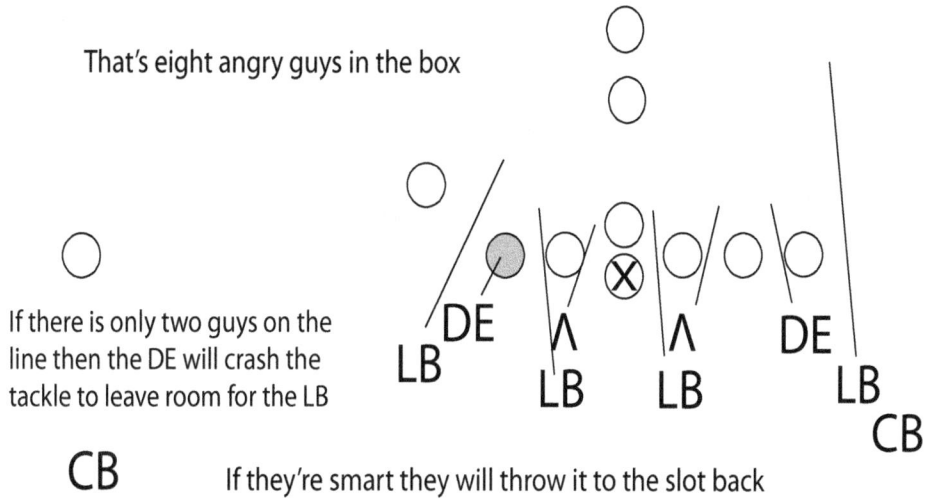

That's eight angry guys in the box

If there is only two guys on the line then the DE will crash the tackle to leave room for the LB

DE   ∧   ∧   DE
LB   LB   LB   LB

CB   CB

CB   If they're smart they will throw it to the slot back

FS

backers second, then the inside linebackers. If they still insist on scoring I will send everybody right side inside left side outside double loops. Now either they scored or we dropped them for a loss. If they are smart they will see we only had three guys playing pass coverage so they will try to pass the ball on the next play. I can take the chance and blitz everyone or I can sit back in coverage, what to do? I will sit back this time and play pass with just a regular defense. If they try to pass the ball I have a good chance to stop it.

When you are blitzing you want to be aware of their alignment as to where the most people are. I was in a game where the other team put four guys on the line left of the center and two in the backfield on the same side of the center and left just two on the other side. I had to shift my guys over to compensate for the off balanced line. When I shift I have them move over one position at a time, so if the left tackle is over the guard he will shift to the center and so on down the line. Sometimes I had to shift more than once to get enough guys on the strong side to stop their sweep. This is why some teams will go with a strong side and weak side alignment on defense so they will have the ability to adjust to any alignment that may be heavy to one side. However in the younger ages you will have to do that

The defensive ends line up on the outside shoulder of the wing back or tight end unless there is a guy split out wide then he will move into the outside shoulder of the tackle

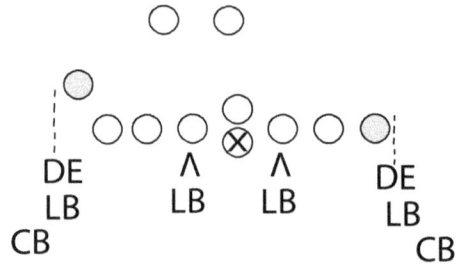

DE LB CB ^ LB LB ^ LB DE LB CB

FS

Shift Right

You may need a linebacker on the field to make the call to shift

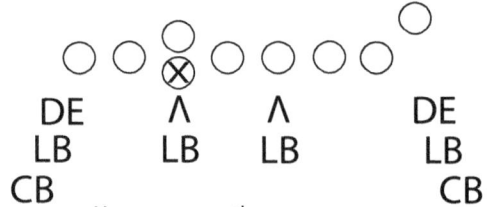

DE LB CB ^ LB LB ^ LB DE LB CB

You can move the safety over if you feel the need

FS

from the sidelines so be aware of it and have that as part of your defense so you can go to it when you need to. If they come out in something you haven't seen before don't panic just set up in your regular defense and spread out evenly across whatever formation they have. You can be ready for this by going over a few different line-ups in practice just to give them a feel for new things. Just stay in your regular defense and again just spread across the formation. You can still run your blitzes they may just

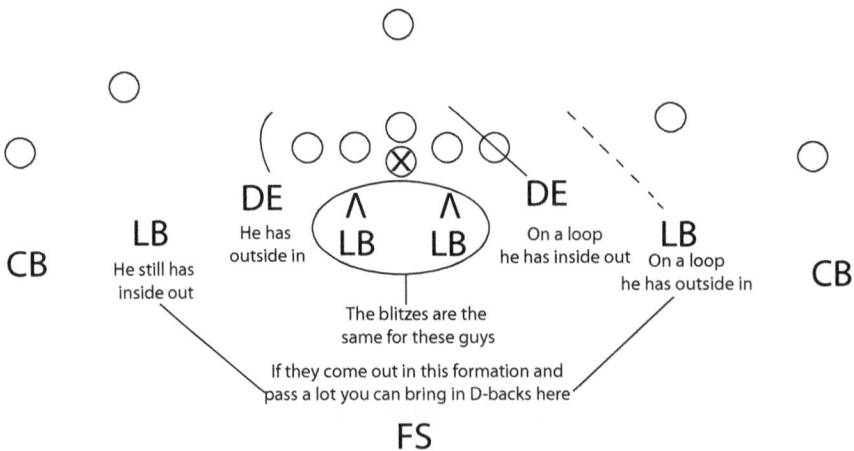

CB LB He still has inside out DE He has outside in ^ LB ^ LB DE On a loop he has inside out LB On a loop he has outside in CB

The blitzes are the same for these guys

If they come out in this formation and pass a lot you can bring in D-backs here

FS

have to come from a little different distance or angle but they will be basically the same.

If you have a team that is old enough to read offensive formations you will want the defensive play caller that is on the field adjust the call as to the alignment as he sees the offensive set. If you want to still run some blitzes from the spread out version of your defense we can take a look at a few ways to do this to give you an idea on how this can be done.

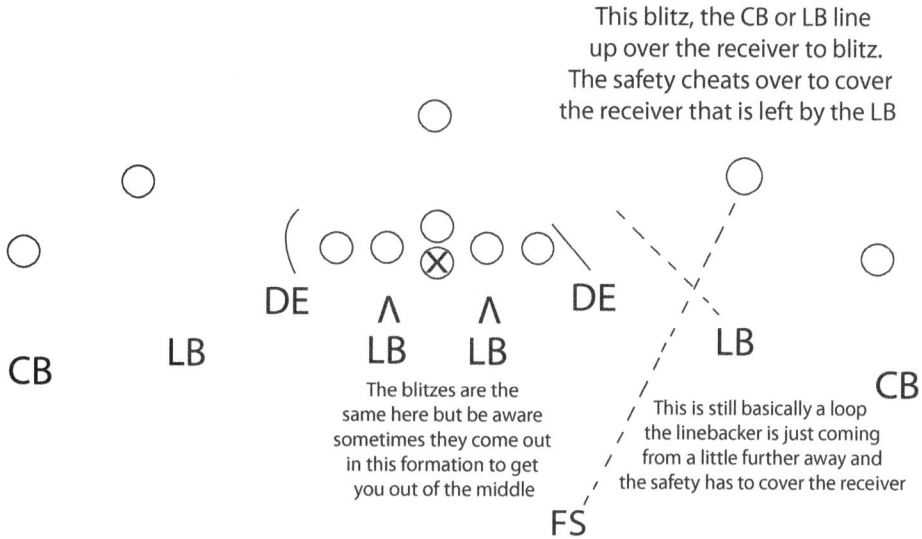

This blitz, the CB or LB line up over the receiver to blitz. The safety cheats over to cover the receiver that is left by the LB

DE   DE
LB   LB   LB   LB
CB

The blitzes are the same here but be aware sometimes they come out in this formation to get you out of the middle

This is still basically a loop the linebacker is just coming from a little further away and the safety has to cover the receiver

CB

FS

If they are smart they will see that the safety has to come over from the middle of the field to cover the receiver. What you can do is after you run it this way first, you can switch the corner back and the safety and have the safety take the wide receiver and the corner back take the slot receiver. Or in other words they play a zone with the corner back taking the outside flat area and the safety taking the deep third with the rest of the defensive backs and linebackers in their regular zone. This is only if they are on a blitz, if not they will stay in their regular zone coverage. Take a look at another blitz from a spread out formation.

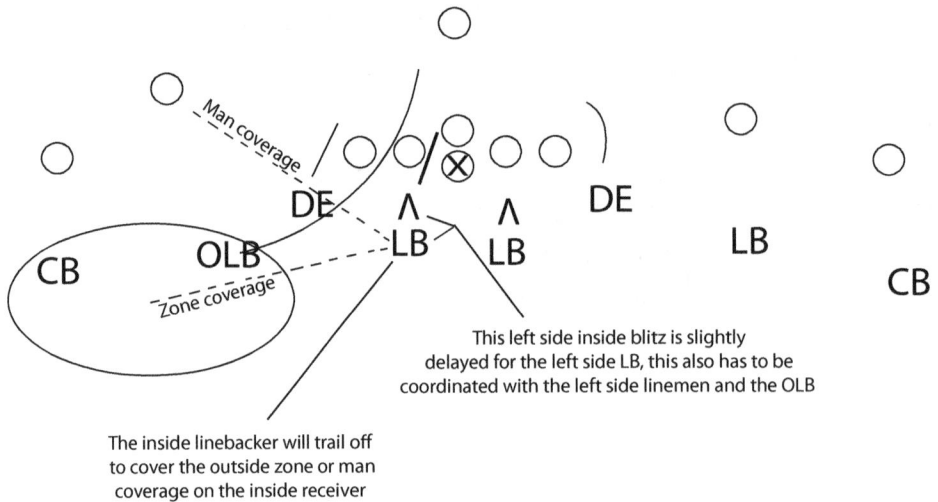

Man coverage

DE

DE

Zone coverage

CB

OLB

LB

LB

LB

CB

This left side inside blitz is slightly delayed for the left side LB, this also has to be coordinated with the left side linemen and the OLB

The inside linebacker will trail off to cover the outside zone or man coverage on the inside receiver

You may also want to be able to call off a blitz if you see something you don't like. That will depend on how the offense lines up. Some teams will have a trick play or two where they will line up weird. I tell my team not to panic just spread yourselves out evenly and take a look at the formation and not so much where the ball is before it's snapped. If the formation is really out there just call a time out and you can make the adjustment. For the most part if the other team is doing a weird play or two that usually means they are desperate and I am forcing them into it. That is a good sign for me.

From the split six I can do a number of things and I will stay in it for as long as it works. I will change things up if I see something that will work better against an opposing team. As I mentioned in an earlier chapter, I played a team with a great runner but that was all they had so I made a little adjustment to the split six and put a man on him fulltime which I called a box in one just like in basketball.

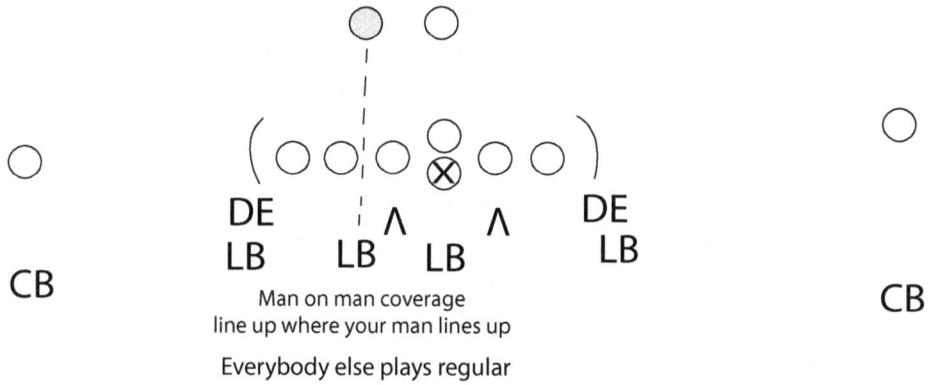

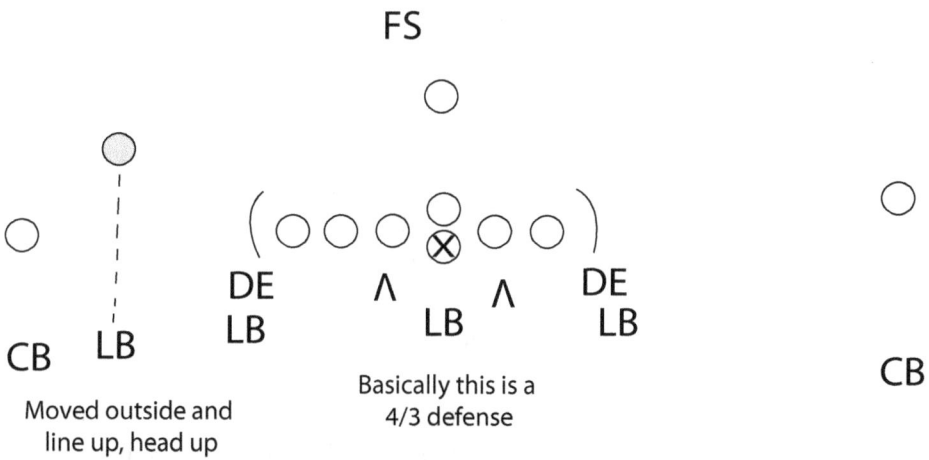

DE   ∧   ∧   DE
LB   LB   LB   LB

CB

Man on man coverage
line up where your man lines up

Everybody else plays regular

CB

FS

DE   ∧   ∧   DE
LB   LB   LB

CB   LB

Basically this is a
4/3 defense

CB

Moved outside and
line up, head up

FS

I didn't change that much but it made a big difference in the game. I remember now that in the second half they made some adjustment trying to compensate for my man-on-man coverage to their great player, so I went back to my regular split six defense. Even though they were a good team I had them on the ropes by then and they were out of their game. So goes the saying "It's sometimes better to be lucky than good." Side note: I had the chance to scout that team so I had all week to prepare for them. I'm not sure I would have made that adjustment in the middle of the game.

I guess the point is you first have to have a good defense to start with, then you can make changes to it or even try something new but it is always a good idea to have your regular defense on line all the time so if you need to you can go back to it and stay in the game.

When you have your plays sharp and ready to go tucked away nicely in your toolbox you can go into a game with confidence knowing you can take advantage of what the other team is doing or not doing. Never panic or lose your cool, you can think a lot better if you can stay calm and assess the situation with a clear head. Don't be afraid to make adjustments, but don't get carried away and make too many that you can't recognize your own program. Stay with what works and don't stop till it does. Set up your next plays and situation so when you are ready you can move to take advantage of what you set up.

Option defense

I would not be a good friend if I didn't at least go over the defense you need against the option. I think I take a little different approach to this than most coaches. I like to get the ball out of the hands of the quarterback and force the pitch quickly or have him turn up field, this way the rest of the team can leave their man and focus on the ball.

When defending the option you have to assign a player to each step of the option and then have a back up on his way. First off I put the defensive end on the quarterback and the outside linebacker on the pitchman, the two linemen and inside linebackers have the dive man first then the linebacker will go to the pitch after he sees that the ball is not with the dive play. The defensive end on the side where the ball is not will play safety to stop any attempt at a reverse.

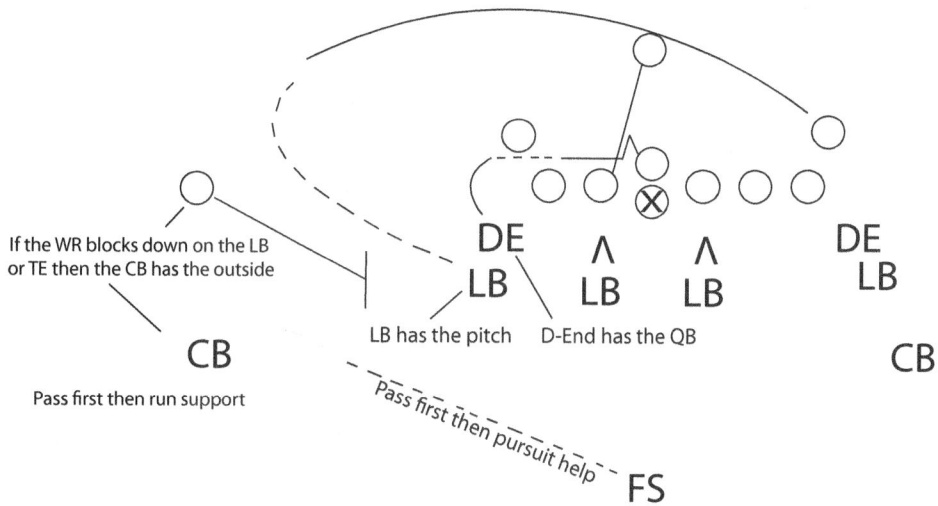

If the WR blocks down on the LB or TE then the CB has the outside

DE

LB

∧ LB

∧ LB

DE

LB

LB has the pitch   D-End has the QB

CB

Pass first then run support

CB

Pass first then pursuit help

FS

I will not have the defensive end wait for the quarterback, I have him go after him as soon as he sees him with the ball, and again I want the quarterback to get rid of the ball or have my defensive end make him eat it. The next thing and this applies to all: "Don't get blocked." The two corners and the safety will stay on pass coverage till the runner, or more so, the ball carrier crosses the line of scrimmage then they come up to help. If the corner back sees the wide receiver crack back block down on the linebacker or defensive end then he will come up on the play and will have outside responsibility.

I am most afraid of this offense because you are so focused on the run you are vulnerable to the pass and if the runner can get loose for a long run and/or a touchdown that will hurt. This offense takes a long time to learn and has to be run so much in practice that it leaves little time for anything else like the passing attack. So they will spend most of the time in practice working on the option and not a lot of time on the passing game, but if they ever find out how to incorporate the pass into this offense this will be an even harder offense to stop. This is why I feel if I can stop their run and get them in a passing situation. I feel like I have them out of their game, and I have the edge. The other thing is if you have the lead the option is a lot harder to come from behind and make up the score. This is because the clock runs a lot more with this type of offense.

Take a look at another way you can run the split six with this defense against the option just to get you thinking of how you can develop your own style of defense for different situations.

Most teams like to force this play to the outside
to allow for help to come from the inside

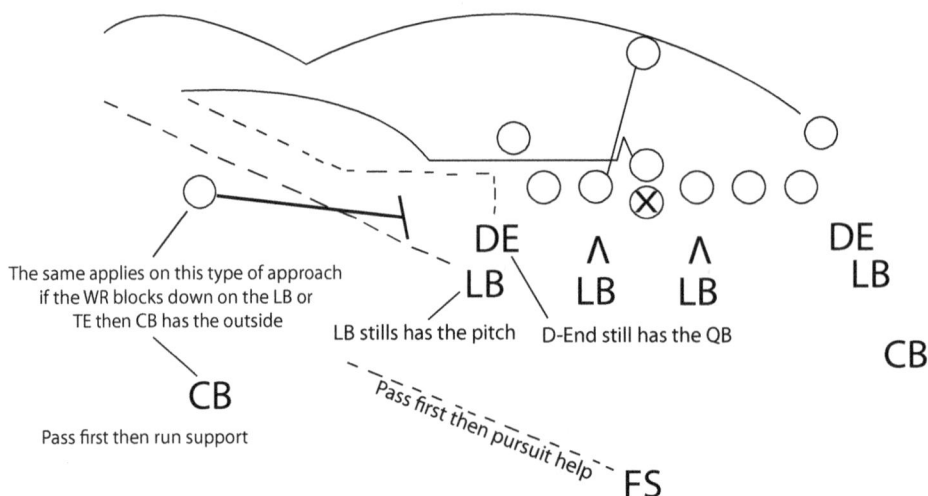

The same applies on this type of approach
if the WR blocks down on the LB or
TE then CB has the outside

DE

LB

LB stills has the pitch   D-End still has the QB

DE
LB

CB

CB

Pass first then run support

Pass first then pursuit help

FS

Special teams

In a game when I hold a team and they have to go into a punt formation I stay in my regular defense or maybe a prevent defense with the exception of the safety. If he can field the ball great, but if not I send in my punt receive guy. I stay in my regular defense because I don't care that much about a great return as much as I want my offense on the field. This goes back to the risk management and percentages that I talked about earlier. I think my offense has a better chance to score than my punt return team so I will have the punt return guy just catch the ball as a fair catch, or if I feel he can think of two things at the same time I will tell him to just go straight and don't worry about being a hero. I am more concerned about a fake punt and a roughing the kicker call over giving up a few more yards, so I like to stay in my regular defense and make sure they kick the ball. I can't tell you how many times I stayed in my split six defense and had the other team call a time out to put their real punt team in. They saw I left my first team defense on the field so they changed their minds. Even the best punt returnees in the country can't get a run back every time, in fact

176

they lose yardage half the time, so for me I think the percentages of failure are too high to take any undue risks. I do however want him to catch the ball and not let it roll for more yards, but if he feels it is out of his reach then just let it go, I can make it back on offense.

Now moving on to another small concept I do a little different than most coaches is the special teams and how I set that up. If I am in the younger ages I will not send in a whole new team for the punt and punt receive. These two special teams are closely related to offense and defense so while I'm on offense and need to punt the ball, I will just use the players that are already on the field with the exception of the punter and then go to a punt formation. That is the only change I make and if the punter is already on the field then I will just switch them around. This works well in the younger ages because a lot of them play both ways and most of them can tackle. You also don't have a lot of extra guys because the league will split the teams up into smaller groups so there is more of a chance for everyone to play. If you are in the higher age groups you will have the luxury of a lot more kids to work with. There will be a few more players and you can get more specific as to whom you want to be on your special teams as far as the ones that more suit your program. To me this is not a dumping ground I want my best players on the field. You can't control where the ball is going to go so if you have a weak player they could easily take advantage of him and that would be bad. On the punt team for instance you will want to use players that are really fast and can make an open field tackle.

Kick off

If I have to kick the ball first in a game I like to go with the open area kick for the kick off and try to recover it. I will try to have the kicker put the ball right in front of my bench. If we get a good kick and it is in the open I start yelling, "Get away from it, get away from it." That will confuse the other team and they think they need to leave it alone, my team knows this is not a punt and will try to recover the ball. Crazy as that sounds it has worked.

If I have a great kicker that can kick the ball into the end zone I will go with that but in the younger ages that is rarely the case so you have to be a little more creative with your kicks. Depending on how young they are they can rarely get the ball past the fifty yard line so that is why I go with the shorter kick to an open area because I feel like they can't kick it that far to start with, so at least I would like a shot at recovering the ball.

The onside kick is also a favorite of mine in the younger ages because you have just as good a chance at recovering the ball as they do and again they can't kick it that far anyway.

Kick receive

On the kick receive I like to go with the miss direction when I can, this is also a chance to take advantage of the youth and inexperience of the players. They will always go towards the ball as the runner starts his return and the defense will leave their lanes. They will also quickly forget about the guys you sent to the other side or the wrong side of the play. Then when they realize after the cutback that you have blockers waiting for them on the cutback side it will be too late and they will be out of position to get back. When they do start their way back they will be met with blockers you sent to the wrong side. Now on the right side of the play or the cutback side you will have blockers waiting to make key blocks. When I am in the lead I will go with the longest kick I can just to eat up more time.

Football Physics

Now that I have had some time to think about the physics of football, let's go back to it for a moment. I didn't major in physics in college so I'm not even sure if this is accurate but there are a few things to consider when thinking about football and what is physically possible.

I was in a game where I had a fast tailback or two back but every time he ran the twenty-eight he would get hit for a minimal gain. As I thought about it I decided that he needed to change his angle to the outside. He was cutting up field too soon and the defensive linebacker would have the angle of pursuit that cut him off as he turned downfield. I told him to run straight to the sidelines and as he ran out of grass then turn up field. He did so and he ran for a touchdown but this play also had a very big detail to it, he was really fast. Just by changing the angle he was able to out run the defense to the sideline and then turn up field so that the defense was now in a catch up mode.

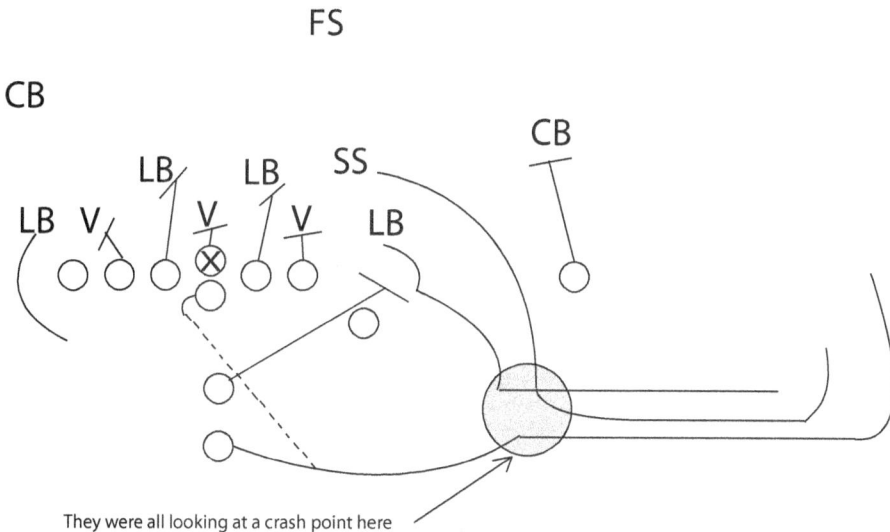

They were all looking at a crash point here

When he took an arching route they drew an angle on him and scheduled a meeting close to the line of scrimmage. When he changed his angle they were unable to catch up with him.

Sometimes the edge is not the answer. With the sweep you can plan a little physics as well. As far as we can tell from this when you run a sweep you are trying to get around the end but sometimes if you don't have that great speed you may want to adjust that slightly to facilitate a cutback. Let's go to the diagram to illustrate this further.

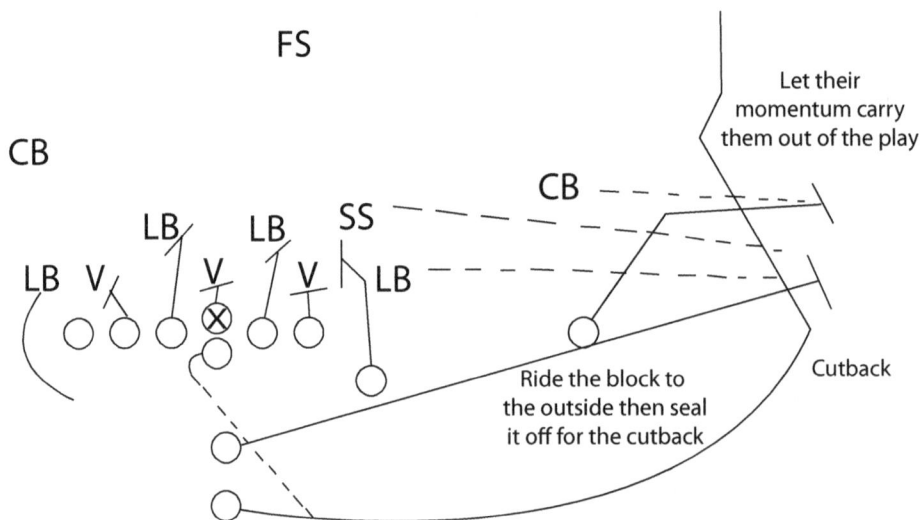

As the runner is drawing his line to get around the end he is running as fast as he can to the edge. On the other side they are getting ready for a meeting with him at the same place, so I would try to reschedule that meeting for a different time by letting their momentum carry them past the runner and out of the play. As you have the runner cutback and take a few new steps to the inside this will open up the lane to head downfield. This is a simple example and something I'm not sure you can teach but I try every year anyway. To sum it up you want to take an angle and then change that angle so the defense has to reset the pursuit, this will help in acquiring more yardage.

The physics of the slant pattern

Pass patterns can also be a matter of physics, let's take a look at some patterns and see what we can see. When I say that the only defender that can stop the slant pattern is the linebacker, that is also a question of physics if it is run right, the defensive back cannot get to the front of the receiver without interfering with the pass. Let's take a look at the diagram and examine it from a physics point of view.

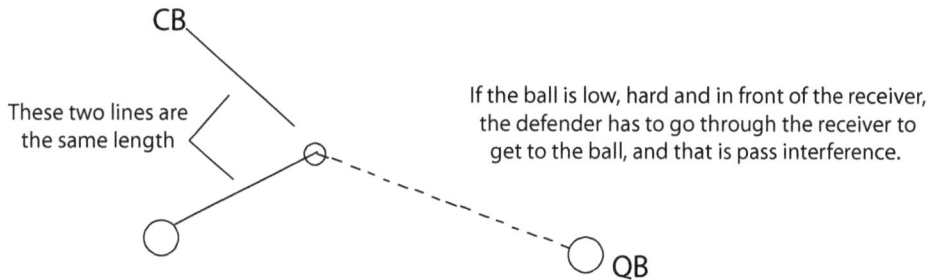

CB

These two lines are the same length

If the ball is low, hard and in front of the receiver, the defender has to go through the receiver to get to the ball, and that is pass interference.

QB

The two lines on the left of the diagram are the same length but you can see that there is a space between the receiver and the defender and that is not taking into account that there was also a half second of reaction time. The defender not only has to make up the difference in space, he has to react to it first. Second the ball is to be thrown in front of the receiver. If that is done then the defender is behind the play and he will have to be super fast to catch up. Also if the receiver catches the ball in full stride then it is very hard for the defender to make the play. In all my years I have only seen one defensive back make this play, but I think it was a case of chemical assistance. For the rest of us it will have to be the linebacker who can come from underneath and get in front of the slant pattern to stop this play. That is also why it works much better in short yardage situations.

The slant pump and go is another case of physics. By the time the defender can stop and start back the receiver is gone.

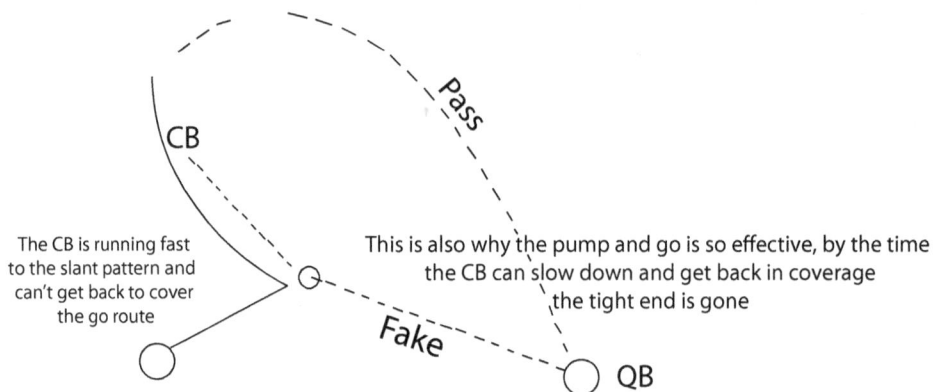

CB

The CB is running fast to the slant pattern and can't get back to cover the go route

Pass

This is also why the pump and go is so effective, by the time the CB can slow down and get back in coverage the tight end is gone

Fake

QB

As a side note, there are many slant patterns you can use, some are deeper and some start out like a streak and cut to the inside like a post but at a sharper angle.

Slant, Slant, Post

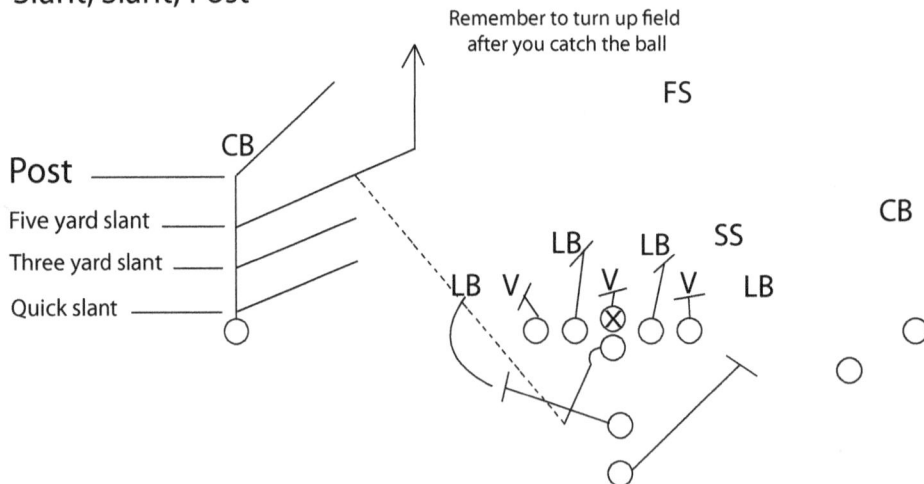

Remember to turn up field after you catch the ball

FS

CB

Post

Five yard slant

Three yard slant

Quick slant

CB

LB   LB   SS

LB V   V   LB

CB

You can run this when the defensive back is further back and his first steps are backwards. Be careful not to go too deep or you will run the risk of the safety coming across and making the play on the ball.

Two places at the same time

The next thing about the physics of football is that you can't be in two places at the same time. If you run a thirty-three the linebackers and defensive backs will come up to defend it. If you run a pass play they will go back into coverage. If you have a play that looks like a run but is really a pass then the linebackers and defensive backs will come up just like they do on a run play and that will leave them out of position to defend the pass.

The last thing is that if you are going in a particular direction it is extremely difficult to quickly go back in the other direction. So if you want more yards then get the bad guys to go in the wrong direction first and then go back to the place they just vacated.

I showed this example a little earlier with the twenty-three cross that is more commonly known as a miss direction play. Go back to it and look at it from a physics point-of-view and see why this play works well against a quick team.

Summation

I hope by now you can see a pattern and a concept start to form in your mind and remember I don't have all the answers, nobody does. That is because it is always changing, you have to understand the basic concepts and then go to what works for you. I run a different program now than just a few years ago so don't think this is the only and cure all for what ails you, it is only the beginning. You have to develop your own program and use what you know best to start with, but don't be afraid to change your mind and move to something better. When you see something that works better, use it. I don't care if you use my plays - I want you to. That is because I am always changing them as I get new and different players that may be better at a particular position, I will adjust to them. If I get a great quarterback I will pass more and if I get a great runner then I will run. If I get them both at the same time I will yell Hallelujah! and go undefeated. (One time I had a great quarterback and no receiver ???) Oh what to do?

Listen to your assistant coaches and team players, they may have seen or done something in the past that works well and all you have to do is adapt it to your own system. Be creative and think how you can take advantage of what the other team is doing or not doing.

Take your big play and build other plays off of it that will make it hard for the other team to know what you are going to do next. Last and probably the most important is to get the other team to do what you want them to do on defense as well as offense, make them play your game by setting them up with the jab to the gut and then hit them with the right cross. Finally have fun, if you are not having fun then go back and sit down in the stands and let someone else take it for a while. This is a fun game and we all should be making sure that happens. Watch, look and listen and you will learn a lot. The Lord gave us two ears and one mouth so we could listen twice as much as we talk, do that.

In the last chapter I put in random thoughts about football, because there is always something new to be learned. Read them and add any of your own then send them to me so I can keep learning as well.

Chapter Eleven
Random thoughts about football

This last chapter is just random thoughts about football and some of the good, bad and the ugly. Let's start with the ugly because I just watched a big name school lose a bowl game on dumbness alone. As I mentioned before I rarely if never play man-on-man on pass coverage but for sure never when there is only seconds left in a game and I am winning. Yet I still watch teams lose every year doing that very thing. With just seconds I think about thirty of them, team "A" I will call them team "A" because I have done dumb things too and I wouldn't want to have my name in this book for doing what I saw them do. So back to team "A" they were ahead and defending about on their thirty-five yard line. They were in a man-on-man coverage when the receiver ran a ten yard slant and the defender went for the ball to knock it down, but was a fraction of a second late and the receiver made the catch and ran for a touchdown. There was no safety help and no help of any kind. Even if he let him catch the ball and made the tackle, it would have taken at least ten seconds to get the next play off and that is if he just spiked it. Not to put it all on one player they were in a man-on-man coverage with under a minute to go, that is how the other team got all the way down to the thirty-five yard line in the first place. They just kept hitting the short pattern, then running for a few more yards before anybody turned around and left their man to help. I am sure they would have won the game if they would have been in a soft zone or what I like to call a prevent defense.

I wanted the other team to win anyway so I didn't mind at the time, but for future sake think, all you have to do is beat one guy in a man-on-man coverage situation; but with zone you have to beat three or more to make a great play and you have help from the safety. If they were in a zone defense and maybe a prevent defense they would have a much better chance to win the game and not give it up so easily. I have never lost when I was leading going into the last minutes of the game. In retrospect I didn't think anything of it at the time but it seems impossible to me now. This may sound a little harsh but the only way you can lose playing zone is with a Hail Mary and I've said a few of those.

You learn more from your losses than your wins, that is why it took me so long.

I agonize over losses. I replay them over and over in my head till I have to take an aspirin and lie down. I don't need to go over film the next day I can't get a loss out of my mind. I will try to find the reasons I did what I did wrong and try to fix it.

Youth football manual from the university of, I already tried that.

Playing everyone

Let me say a few words about playing everyone. There is a way to do this without hurting the team or your not so good players. Yes the starters are the best players you have, but the back ups are just as important. You want them to get better and have fun and of course keep the parents off your back.

I always have my best players on the field on defense because you can't control where the ball is going to go, but you can on offense. That is where I try to get all the players in the game. I can control where and what play I want to run so I will put in the players that might be a little weak in spots where they can do well and not hurt the team. This will give them game time on the field and help them to improve. You also want to do it early so that when you are in the last quarter and the score is tied you will be able to not have to worry about the guys you still need to play.

When I want to bring in a back up I will tell the starter that he is doing a great job and I just want to give some of the other players a turn on the field. Starters always feel like they should never be taken out of a game for any reason some look at that as a big thing. If you approach it as I showed you it will give them a better outlook and they will understand. I had a wide receiver one time that was small and I was afraid he would get hurt, so I was careful to put him in only on running plays. On this one play the runner did a cutback to his side and this little kid made a key block on the defensive back and the play went for more yards. I thought to myself, "Hey that could work." I started to put him in on plays that went to his side and he would always make the right block. As a reward I even threw the ball to him a few times but he never caught it. The point is I found a talent he had (maybe by accident) and used it to help both of us. Everyone on the team slapped him on the back every time he made the block and gave him his well-deserved "good job".

Positive reinforcement

During a game you need to take all the blame for everything that goes wrong and give praise for everything that goes right. We are not dealing with million dollar athletes, these are just kids and they are very impressionable. They can get down easily and just do worse. Always be positive and build them up, if you take the blame for the bad they will try to do better just to help you.

Small adjustments only

Do not try to make big wholesale changes during a game if they didn't get it during the weeks of practice they are not going to get it during a game. I have seen coaches move players to a different position in the middle of a game and expect them to do well. If he can't make a tackle as a linebacker he is not going to do it as a defensive end. I have moved players around before but rarely in the middle of a game, which will always be a case-by-case call. I did it when I had a week to teach him what I wanted. I did it because they had one running back that did everything on their team. Wherever he went that is where the ball went. I put my best player, who was the left side linebacker on him and told him to line up wherever he lined up and go wherever he goes. I made an adjustment with the other linebacker and moved him to the middle of the formation to compensate for the missing left side linebacker. That shut down their offense for a while till they figured out what we did but they really couldn't do a lot more because they relied too much on one guy. This is also a very good example for why you want to develop lesser players so you will not just be a one-man show. They had a great jab, but no right cross. I like to hide that guy or play or what I like to call, my right cross, till I need a big down. Now late in the game when I need a big play I can pull out the big gun and they have no time to adjust.

Punting the ball to their best guy?

Punt the ball out of bounds. You will never get a run back for a touchdown or long run ever. Until they change the rule never kick it to their best guy or to anybody that can run it back. Are you kidding? Why? I will never understand this call. So you give up a few yards you will never give up a score if you punt the ball out of bounds. I don't mean a ten-yard punt I mean as far as you can, but at an angle to the side furthest away from the receiver. I will give you just one of many, for instance. I was the assistant coach in charge of the sophomore team so during the varsity games I was just there. We were in a game with a bitter rival and backed up on are twenty-yard line we had a small lead and time was short. I suggested he go with a quick kick, but he didn't have one. So after a third and short went nowhere I said don't punt it to him he is their best runner, kick it long and out of bounds. My advice was ignored and they kicked it to him and he ran it back for a game winning touchdown. Not only was it a bad idea, it gave them a lift to sustain their lead and it took the wind out of us and we couldn't recover. Why? Why? Why? Would you ever kick it to guy who can run well or even great if you don't have to? The only thing I can think of is that you have an ego that needs love. If kicking the ball out of bounds on the kick off team were legal that would be one of my plays. Here let's kick it to the best runner in the state, see if you can run it back on me. Or, you want the ball kid? It's over there in the Gatorade, go get it.

FYI

Just a little note for the FYI section of your program, take some time with each position and focus on that spot and all that goes with it. You can show the coaches and the players all the ins and outs and how you want that position to perform and how it plays into your program. This is also a very good time to focus and give some real detail work with each position; I don't like to spend time with the quarterbacks while the linemen all stand around and watch. That is why it is so important to have assistant coaches. They can take their team and give them specific training relative to that position, while you do the same with yours. So go over each position with that coach in advance and make sure he knows what you want. Then leave them alone and let them work, you can oversee their progress when you are all together and then make adjustments at the next meeting.

I don't claim to know a lot about line blocking, I leave that up to the line coach. I make sure he knows what it is I want from the linemen, and then I let him do whatever he needs. As long as he gets the job done I don't care and don't want to know how every little thing is done. I can't be watching him every moment and I don't want to, I want to trust him and let him do his job.

I am open to everything but just because I will listen that doesn't mean I will do it. However I remember a time when I was showing the linemen and the coach what I wanted to have happen on a particular pass rush. I was working on it for the next team we were about to play. The team I was about to play threw the ball a lot and so we needed a bigger pass rush. As I was explaining what I wanted, one of the linemen stepped forward and wanted to run it differently than I wanted. I stepped back and told him to show me. He did, then the line coach and I looked at each other and said, "OK! That will work." He just did one of the prettiest swim moves I have ever seen. I looked back at the line coach and said. "I'm going back over to the linebackers now." And I left them to their work, letting them spend the rest of the time teaching that move to all of the linemen. Sometimes you don't know it all or even know what players and coaches are capable of. You need to just let them do it their way. Leaders step up, stars are born and people become more than you ever thought they could, all this because you gave them the room to work. These little successes will help build your team up, if you let them. Be patient and give room for growth. You don't have to know it all you just have to know where to find it. Leave the door open and let the creativity fly between people, sometimes you have to step back just to keep from getting run over.

This is probably not all you need to know but it is a good start. The key is to realize that you can't know it all. When you come to that realization it opens the door and allows more to come to you. If and only if you keep your mind open and listen and watch you will learn more and become a better coach; you will have more fun and sleep better at night. There is always a better way and it is not always yours.

Random thought

"The weaker you are on the line the more you have to finesse" Lou Holtz. Another thing Lou Holtz said when he talked about announcers, "The trick is to keep talking until you think of something to say." Keep that in mind when you are watching a game and never take anything they say as fact. I love announcers but it's just one man's opinion just like mine. It has to come from you for it to mean anything. My hope is that you just start thinking and creating.

Too cool for school

If you have a member of your team who thinks he is the most important and that without him you will never make it, you have to change his mind by letting him see that he can't do it alone and that is easy, just let him try it alone.

I had this very situation a few years ago and told him that if he was so good, here's the ball do it. He turned to me with a look of "yeah right" so I said, "Oh do you want a few more guys on your side?" He replied with a yes and we went on from there.

Cancer in the ranks

The quarterback is the most important player on the team but he also can't do it alone. A quarterback that thinks he can will drag the rest of the team down and make it hard to move forward. That will go for any player that has a bad attitude. It will work like a cancer and destroy your team. If I ever hear a team member put down another team member or coach I take that as a very serious issue. That can start a landside and again destroy your team from the inside. I stop practice and make sure that they know that is not acceptable and that he can go home to mommy if he doesn't like it. In addition a player that thinks more about his numbers and stats and not the team will come back to bite you in the back side. When you get in a close game and he doesn't want to throw the ball because he doesn't want an incomplete pass on his stats and would rather takes the sack thinking that will be the linemen's fault. You may want to rethink the move and try the next guy. He may be a great quarterback but he is not a great player, like the miracle hockey team coach for the Olympics said, "I am not looking for the best players I'm looking for the right players." The best players are not going to save you if they are not on the same team as the rest of your players.

The right attitude is gold

If you want them to be champions then start treating them as such telling them that a champion will always put his team first and always try to uplift and not drag down his teammates. A champion always shows good sportsmanship and helps the other team to their feet after they knock him down. They never say we can't they will say and believe we can. They will get the right attitude from you "their leader". That is why winning teams keep winning, like I said before winners are winners, and losers are losers, that is because neither one wants to be around the other, it makes them uncomfortable.

Mommy has to go back to the stands

I had a tight end that thought he was irreplaceable and started to act like it. I benched him and put the wide receiver in his spot. His mother came to me and wanted to know what the heck I was doing. I told her and she understood and gave me her support, the next game and from then on he was the best tight end I ever had, player and attitude.

You have to maintain control and that goes for the coaches as well. If you have a bad seed you must take action and that means dismissing if you have to. If a parent or assistant coach says, "I'll take my son with me if I go", tell him the kid can stay, he can't. I never punish the players for their parents. Remember it's about the kids. Mommy and daddy have to go back to the stands.

One voice, one leader

I also do not believe in the two-quarterback system. I feel the team has to trust the leader and not get confused as to who is in charge. I will say that I do like the way the University of Utah and Florida do it with their direct snap to a running back, but I feel like that is more of a play rather than a new quarterback.

The University of Utah beat the Crimson Tide in a bowl game that nobody saw coming. A team that was bigger by about forty pounds per player. The insightful announcers said at the beginning of the game, "They won't be able to run on them". They were right they didn't need to. The University of Utah passed the ball on almost every down. They went down the field in three consecutive series and were up twenty-one to zero in the first quarter. How did they do that you ask? They took what they were given and used it well. By the time Alabama knew what hit them they were playing catch up and it was too little too late. You can beat a better team, you just have to be better on that day yourself, don't fight it, take what they give you and always say thanks.

Tools and how to use them

Tool number one, the big hammer or what I like to call the (slot right twenty-four). Take the big hammer and hit your opponent with it a few times, then take the little hammer (Slot right twenty-four quarterback keeper) and tap him on the forehead once. Now that you have his attention hit him again with the big hammer. Now take out the big hammer and set it down so he can see it, then take one of your smaller more precise tools and slice off an ear or something small (twenty-three cross). Now hit him with the big hammer a few more times. Then just repeat big one, little one then the big one again. Now that you have him in the corner whimpering and his eyes are red, he can't see straight. Now is the time to hit him with the very sharp surgical knife - to the heart (twenty-four bootleg). This is the basic concept of football or any team against team sport for that matter. Just mix it up a little to keep them on their heels.

The Football Coaching Bible by the American Football Association © by Human Kinetics, Inc.

Lou Holtz talk given in San Diego at an investment seminar.

www.ingramcontent.com/pod-product-compliance
Lightning Source LLC
Chambersburg PA
CBHW080934040426
42443CB00015B/3412